Please return/renew this item by the last date shown.
Items may also be renewed by the internet*

https://library.eastriding.gov.uk

* Please note a PIN will be required to access this service
- this can be obtained from your library

TINY
CHURCHES

DIXE WILLS

Published by AA Publishing, a trading name of AA Media Limited,
Fanum House, Basing View, Basingstoke, Hampshire, RG21 4EA, UK.

theAA.com

First published in 2016. Reprinted 2017 (twice).
This paperback edition published October 2018
10 9 8 7 6 5 4

A CIP catalogue record for this book is available from the British Library.

ISBN: 978-0-7495-7991-3

Editor: Donna Wood
Art Director: James Tims
Designer: Liz Baldin
Image retouching and internal repro: Ian Little

Printed and bound in China by 1010 Printing International

A05642

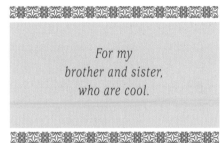

*For my
brother and sister,
who are cool.*

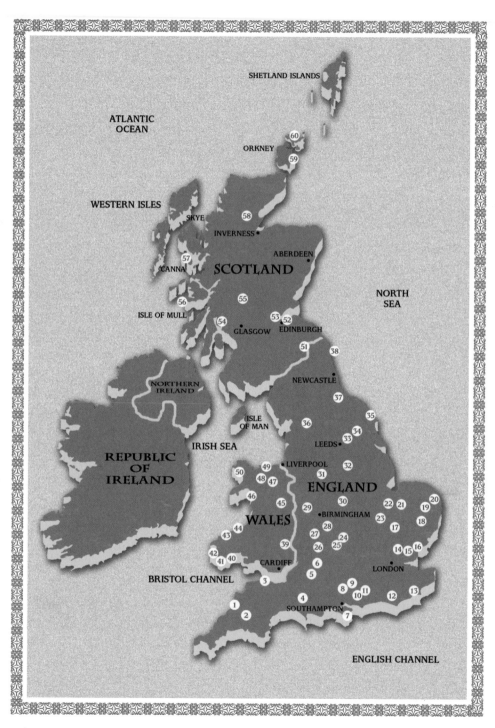

SHETLAND ISLANDS

ATLANTIC
OCEAN

ORKNEY

60

59

WESTERN ISLES

SKYE

58

INVERNESS

CANNA

57

ABERDEEN

SCOTLAND

NORTH
SEA

55

56

ISLE OF MULL

54

53 52

GLASGOW   EDINBURGH

51

38

NEWCASTLE

37

NORTHERN
IRELAND

35

ISLE
OF MAN

36

LEEDS 33 34

IRISH SEA

REPUBLIC
OF
IRELAND

50 49   LIVERPOOL

31 32

48 47

ENGLAND

46

45

30

29 BIRMINGHAM

22 21 20

WALES

19

23

18

28

17

44

27 24

43

39

26 25

14

42   40

6

15 16

41

CARDIFF

5

LONDON

3

BRISTOL CHANNEL

8 9

4

10 11

12 13

7

SOUTHAMPTON

ENGLISH CHANNEL

1

2

6

CONTENTS

INTRODUCTION

It was during a recent visit to Canada that it struck me once again how lucky the British are to live among such an abundance of well-preserved ancient churches. While stocking up on a few essentials, I asked the shopkeeper what the principal tourist attractions were in what was quite a large Canadian town. 'Well, if you see only one thing, make sure it's the church,' he replied, before adding in a tone brimming with parochial pride, 'It dates all the way back to the 1920s, you know.'

I put on a suitable show of admiration at this feat of longevity and left before he asked me the date of the oldest church in my home town. Had I tried to downplay the fact that even the nondescript village I grew up in sported a 12th-century church by adding that it was, 'Quite late 12th century,' I would, I fear, still have cut a figure as a thoroughgoing braggart.

What is perhaps all the more extraordinary about the treasure trove of historical architecture in Britain is that a large number of small and insignificant churches has managed to survive into the 21st century, often having weathered several plagues, the Reformation, plummeting attendances and the tender ministrations of the Victorians.

For me, there's something particularly attractive about these ecclesiastical underdogs. They are seldom caught making a grandiose political statement about the power of a particular regime (cf Durham Cathedral booming out, 'We Normans are in power now'). Very few were built to prove that some diocese was richer than its neighbour, or, if they were, they weren't very convincing evidence of it. Yet many make up for their lack of stature with rich decoration, an unorthodox design that sets them apart from the rank and file, or simply a beauty intrinsic in their miniaturised form.

The earliest British churches would have been very small affairs indeed. Many, like St Andrew's at Greensted (p78), began life as basic wooden shelters from which missionaries would preach while their congregation was ranged about them at the mercy of the weather. Even self-styled cathedrals such as the early Saxon St Peter-on-the-Wall in Essex (p88) are mere chapels by today's standards.

Of course, by no means all the churches in this book are ancient. The most recent (St Fursey's, p106) was built in 1998 and other fine examples such as Canna Rhu Church in the Hebrides (p293) and the Friends Meeting House at Dolobran (p231) prove that the art of creating aesthetically pleasing sacred buildings was not lost when the last medieval mason cut his final stone.

When it comes to declaring which place of worship holds the coveted title of Britain's Smallest Church, the waters are somewhat muddied. While Bremilham Church in Wiltshire (p38), which measures a mere 13ft by 11ft, is technically the most diminutive, only one service a year is celebrated there, with the congregation actually sitting outside. Britain's smallest truly active church is thus St Trillo's in Rhos-on-Sea (p251), on the North Wales coast. This holds two services a week despite only having room for half a dozen seats. Deserving of special commendation in this context is the aforementioned St Fursey's, an Antiochan Orthodox church in a Norfolk back garden (p106), where nearly 30 services are conducted each week in a space not much larger than a bus shelter. Meanwhile, the nation's smallest parish church is almost certainly the beguiling St Beuno's, lost in the woods near the coast of North Somerset and only accessible on foot (p26).

On my research trips around the country, from Cornwall up to Orkney, it was a joy to meet older congregants who could perhaps slip me some interesting snippet that didn't appear in the guide. On one occasion, for example, I happened to visit the exquisite Norman Chapel at Durham University at the same time as an elderly alumnus from that august seat of learning. Contrary to official histories, which declare that the long abandoned room was recognised as an ancient chapel during World War II and reconsecrated soon afterwards, he told me that during his time at the university in the 1950s it was being used as a bike shed.

I should make clear that this is by no means a definitive work, in that I have not included every single British church that might be considered tiny. (Nor have I included former church buildings that have been entirely given over to some other function, such as a private dwelling or museum.) Instead I have chosen only those churches which, in my view, are interesting in some way beyond the mere peculiarity of their size. You may, of course, have just cast your eye down the table of contents and exclaimed, 'I can't believe he hasn't included [insert your favourite bijou church here]. I shall write a letter of indignation and disgust to my MP to see if we can't get this poorly researched piece of nonsense banned.'

Just before you reach for your best Basildon Bond though, there may be a reason why I have excluded little St Brigid's-on-the-Swamp or wherever. It may simply be that, although small, I have not deemed it tiny; or, though fetching, it may not be terribly remarkable.

That said, if, despite the months I have spent combing the country, the contents of the British Library and the nether reaches of cyberspace, I have somehow failed to alight upon the diminutive and fascinating gem you hold dear to your heart, try not to take it personally. You can always share your knowledge with me by contacting me via the publishers of this book or by going all 21st century and sending me a tweet (@dixewills).

A few notes about the information contained within these pages. With regards to the 'Spiritual Orientation' of each church, I've taken it as read that those places of worship marked 'Church of England' that were built before Henry VIII's split from Rome would have been Roman Catholic up to that point.

Readers should note that although I have checked the service times of every one of those churches that is still active, these are apt to change, particularly where irregular or infrequent. If you wish to attend a service, do double-check that it's going ahead on the date and time stated.

Conversely, it's also possible that you'll arrive at a church marked in this book as having no services to find a wedding or a christening going on. This is because many apparently redundant churches actually remain consecrated and earn something towards their keep by occasionally being thrust back into the ecclesiastical role for which they were built. If you do hazard upon such an event, see it as a bonus, for you are witnessing the church roused momentarily from its slumber and almost certainly dressed in its best bib and tucker.

With regards to the style of this book, I have tried my best to ensure that the review of each church is not a litany of trefoiled-this and reticulated-that. As is the case with any slightly arcane subject, there is a temptation to exclude outsiders by employing the esoteric vocabulary that goes with it, but I have attempted to write this book in such a way as to make the understanding of churches accessible to all.

However, it is nigh on impossible to avoid using some of the technical expressions that describe church architecture and furnishings. Naturally, you may be perfectly at home with such terminology and speak of little else over the dinner table but your predilection for crocketed ogee arches. If, nonetheless, you're apt to mix up your reredos with your rood screen, there's a glossary at the back of the book (p312) to turn to for enlightenment, as well as an illustration showing the names of the typical features of a church on pp12–13. Consult the table (right) if you need reassurance on the names of the various architectural periods and the dates each covers.

Some newcomers may also find all the talk of east windows, south transepts and north aisles a little disorientating at first. However, things become much easier when you remember that, with very few exceptions (e.g. St Peter's, Linlithgow, p272), the altar will be at the east end of the church. Thus, if you are facing the altar, anything behind you is to the west, anything to your left is north and anything to your right is south.

Finally, I should make it clear that in no circumstances would I dare to call myself an expert on churches. I am but an enthusiastic aficionado with a lifetime's experience of poking around in them and hungrily sifting through the leaflets and magazines on the table by the door for those hallowed sheets of paper entitled 'A Brief Guide to the Church of St...' My hope in writing this book is that you derive as much pleasure from visiting these bijou places of worship – either physically or by means of these pages – as I have done.

Dixe Wills
February 2016

ARCHITECTURAL PERIODS
(as applied principally to England)

Saxon	7th century to 1066
Norman	1066 to 1189
Early English	1189 to 1280
Decorated	1280 to 1377
Perpendicular	1377 to 1547
Early Tudor	1500 to 1547
Late Tudor	1547 to 1603
Stuart (Jacobean & Carolean)	1603 to 1689*
Hanoverian (William & Mary, Anne and Georgian)	1689 to 1837
Specifically Georgian	1714 to 1830
Victorian	1837 to 1901

Technically the period from 1649 to 1660 should not be counted as Stuart, since Charles I was beheaded in 1649 and Charles II did not regain the throne until 1660. However, this is seldom taken into account.

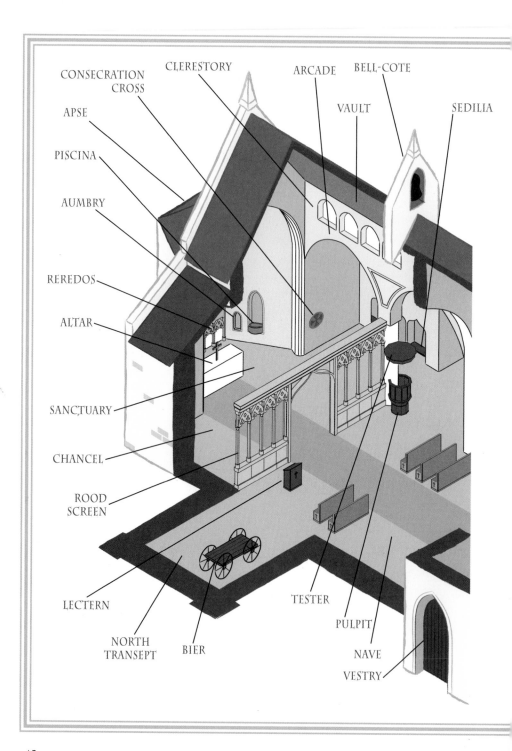

CONSECRATION CROSS

CLERESTORY

ARCADE

BELL-COTE

APSE

VAULT

SEDILIA

PISCINA

AUMBRY

REREDOS

ALTAR

SANCTUARY

CHANCEL

ROOD SCREEN

LECTERN

NORTH TRANSEPT

BIER

TESTER

PULPIT

NAVE

VESTRY

12

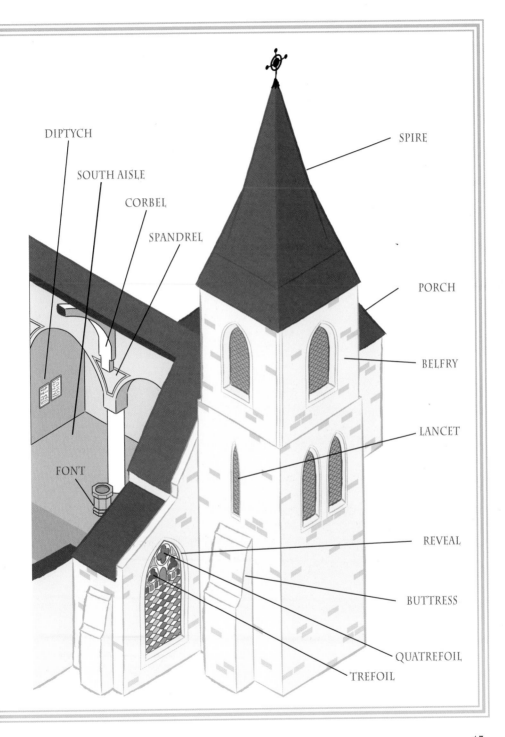

DIPTYCH

SOUTH AISLE

CORBEL

SPANDREL

FONT

SPIRE

PORCH

BELFRY

LANCET

REVEAL

BUTTRESS

QUATREFOIL

TREFOIL

13

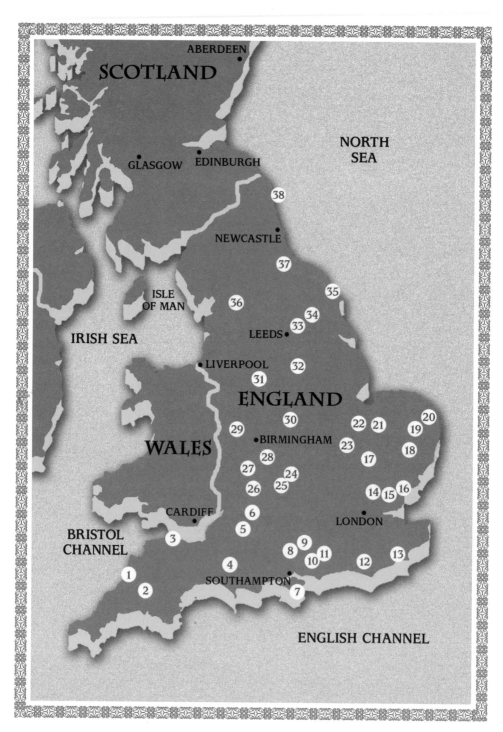

ABERDEEN

SCOTLAND

NORTH SEA

GLASGOW ● EDINBURGH

38

NEWCASTLE

37

35

ISLE OF MAN

36

34

33

IRISH SEA

LEEDS

32

● LIVERPOOL

31

ENGLAND

30

22 21

20

29

19

● BIRMINGHAM

23

17

18

WALES

28

27

24

14 15 16

26

25

CARDIFF

6

LONDON

BRISTOL CHANNEL

3

5

8 9

1

4

10 11

13

2

SOUTHAMPTON

7

12

ENGLISH CHANNEL

ENGLAND

1 Our Lady & St Anne's, Widemouth Bay

2 St Michael of the Rock, Brentor

3 St Beuno's, Culbone

4 St Edwold's, Stockwood

5 St Laurence's, Bradford-on-Avon

6 Bremilham Church, Malmesbury

7 St Lawrence Old Church, St Lawrence

8 St Swithun-upon-Kingsgate, Winchester

9 Old Church of St Mary the Virgin, Preston Candover

10 St Hubert's, Idsworth

11 St Mary's, North Marden

12 Church of the Good Shepherd, Lullington

13 St Thomas Becket, Fairfield

14 St Andrew's, Greensted

15 St Mary's, Mundon

16 St Peter-on-the-Wall, Bradwell-on-Sea

17 St Peter's, Cambridge

18 St Andrew's, Frenze

19 All Saints, Keswick

20 St Fursey's, Sutton

21 St Mary's, Barton Bendish

22 Guyhirn Chapel, Guyhirn

23 St John's, Little Gidding

24 All Saints, Shorthampton

25 St Oswald's, Widford

26 St Mary of the Angels, Brownshill

27 Odda's Chapel, Deerhurst

28 All Saints, Billesley

29 Langley Chapel, Ruckley

30 St Mary's, Snibston

31 Milldale Chapel, Milldale

32 Steetley Chapel, Steetley

33 St Mary's, Lead

34 St Ethelburga's, Great Givendale

35 St Leonard's, Speeton

36 St Leonard's, Chapel-le-Dale

37 Norman Chapel, Durham Castle

38 St Cuthbert's Chapel, Inner Farne

OUR LADY & ST ANNE'S
WIDEMOUTH BAY

Seek out the lovely embroidery depicting St Anne and her daughter, the Virgin Mary.

SPIRITUAL ORIENTATION
Church of England

PHYSICAL ORIENTATION
Leverlake Road, Widemouth Bay, Cornwall EX23 0AB
Grid reference: SS 202 020
OS Landranger map 190

PUBLIC TRANSPORT
Since nearby Bude lost its railway station in 1966, Widemouth Bay has been an awkward place to get to by public transport. The least complicated way is to make for Barnstaple railway station (gwr.com; 0345 7000125) and take the 319 bus to Northgate Green, Hartland, followed by the 219 to Bude. From the seaside resort it's a 3-mile walk to the church on Leverlake Road, almost opposite Coombe Lane. Alternatively you can take the 595 bus from Bude to Widemouth Bay (all three buses stagecoachbus.com; 01392 427711).

OPENING ARRANGEMENTS
Always open.

SERVICES
8am (sometimes 8.30am) Sunday (Holy Communion) – no service on 3rd Sunday
8.30am Wednesday (Holy Communion)
5pm Friday (Evening Service)
Check Sunday service times with churchwarden Judy MacDonald (01288 362254).

While there are many churches around the country that are considered moving, there are very few that have actually been physically picked up and moved. Yet this is precisely what happened to Our Lady and St Anne's. It's perhaps just as well then that it's constructed of wood (though, less happily, its other major constituent is asbestos).

Standing about 300yd from the beach, on the outskirts of a little village near the popular resort of Bude, the church has no pretensions to grandeur and could easily be mistaken by the passer-by for a large white shed, an image reinforced by the garden with pleasant lawns in which it is set. Its only flourish is a tiny cross above a heartbreakingly diminutive bell-cote that harbours a single small bell. For all that, it must be said that the church exudes a ramshackle charm that it could not have attained had it been built of stone.

It's heartening too that even though Our Lady and St Anne's is less than a hundred years old, a cloud of ambiguity hangs over certain aspects of its history. While the local deanery website and a notice inside the church agree that it was built in 1929 as a private oratory in Madeira Drive (at the other end of the village), the former states that it was created for three brothers called Claude, Frank and Reginald Kingdon, who were all priests; the latter maintains that it was built for 'Miss Kirby and Miss Topham who lived at St Anne's'. The church notice further claims that its priest was Reverend James William Hooton, serving under a rural dean called Rev Claude Kingdon.

However, the website does give some biographical detail to back up its assertion, stating that Claude (rector of Whitstone), Frank (rector of Bridgerule) and Reginald (vicar of St John's, Isle of Dogs, London), who all worked into their ninth decade, had the habit of repairing to the oratory for the month of August each year to prepare all their sermons for the following 11 months. All three could then preach the same sermon on the same day wherever they were, thus forming their own micro broadcasting company. Of course, it also meant that each brother was only obliged to compose a third of his own sermons, which was a crafty move.

According to the current owner of St Anne's, the bungalow from whose garden the church was extracted, the oratory was actually built for Miss Kirby and Miss Topham but the two women allowed the Kingdon brothers to use it each August, having been on friendly terms with Frank, whose Bridgerule parish was not so distant.

A fact over which there is no dispute is that the builder of the oratory, a Mr

Bight, moved it from Madeira Drive to its present location in 1940 in order that it might serve as a chapel of ease for local people. Widemouth (pronounced 'Widmuth') had expanded dramatically as a seaside resort in the 1930s and, before the relocation and conversion of the oratory, the burgeoning population had to struggle to the parish church of St Winwaloe's at Poundstock.

The church is laid out in the traditional cruciform shape, though this is rather hamstrung when seen from inside by the fact that one transept has been partitioned off for use as a vestry. It's bright, cheery and airy, despite the low roof, and its chairs are ordered in a few neat rows, with space for just two seats on either side of a carpeted aisle. The impermanent materials with which it is built cry out that this must be a non-conformist place of worship – perhaps an Elim Chapel or some obscure non-denominational outpost – so it's a surprise to find that the church is not only Anglican but really rather High Anglican. There's the reference to the mother and grandmother of Jesus Christ in its name, of course, backed up by a statue of Mary holding her baby son.

The most beautiful object in the church also has a distinctly Catholic edge to it. Framed and hanging on the wall is an embroidery of St Anne pointing at something in a book held by her equally behaloed child, Mary, who also found a certain degree of fame. This was part of a larger piece of material used as the altar front when the church was in Madeira Drive. When it began to show signs of wear this central image was cut out and framed.

Back outside, there's no graveyard, and among the rosemary and lavender stands a flourishing palm, a reminder that we are in the mild climes of Cornwall. However, the church is not the only building in the garden. Rather unexpectedly, there is also a small wooden summerhouse built by members of the congregation in 2006 and often used for local community meetings. It's a charming addition perfectly in keeping with the homely church it serves. 🐾

ST MICHAEL OF THE ROCK

BRENTOR

Enjoy the magnificent sight of the church from below before losing yourself completely in the wonderful atmosphere of serenity within.

SPIRITUAL ORIENTATION

Church of England

PHYSICAL ORIENTATION

Brentor, Tavistock, Devon
PL19 0NP
Grid reference: SX 470 803
OS Landranger map 201

PUBLIC TRANSPORT

From Plymouth railway station (gwr.com; 0345 700 0125) take the 46 bus (plymouthbus.co.uk; 01752 662271) to North Brentor, from where it's a mile's stroll to the church. Walk west out of the village to the T-junction at Yellands where you turn left, eventually taking a left fork below the church – there's a footpath on the left from the road up the tor.

OPENING ARRANGEMENTS

Always open. Audio tours are available to visitors who have downloaded the Viewpoynt app.

SERVICES

6pm Sunday (Easter to Michaelmas unless weather dire) Evensong (except at Easter and Michaelmas when Communion is celebrated)
Carol concert with the Canticoram Singers – normally 1st Sunday in December
3pm Christmas Day Carol Service
Contact churchwarden David Harris for further details (01822 810845).

St Michael's is an excellent example of the difference between Gothic as an architectural style and Gothic as it exists in the popular imagination. The view from beneath the lofty tor on which this little church stands is one that inspires awe and, when the scene is sheathed in fog, perhaps something close to dread too, for this is Dartmoor at its eerie best. The exaggerated squeak of the gate that guards the porch, the clang of the church door as it closes behind you and the feeble guttering light emitted by the gas lamps only add to the drama. The west front is just 3ft from the edge of a cliff, its crenellated tower – struck by lightning in 1994 – is 32ft high and lowers over the land below. It is no wonder that this is a church beset by legends in which the Devil plays a central role.

The church, also known as St Michael de Rupe, was built around 1130 by Robert Giffard, Lord of the Manor of Lamerton and Whitchurch. It may well have served initially as a chantry – a place where a member of the clergy would be paid to celebrate masses for the founder's soul.

The building is 1,150ft above sea level and constructed on the summit of a section of a volcanic cone. The site was an important one long before Giffard's time though, as the remains of an Iron Age hill-fort surrounding the tor demonstrate. Furthermore, during church restoration works carried out in 1889 by the 9th Duke of Bedford, 40 skeletons were discovered beneath the floor. Interestingly, only one was laid east to west, as one might expect in a Christian burial. All the others were laid north to south, as is more customary in pagan rites.

There are three separate tales about how the church came to be built on the tor. The one that has the greatest chance of containing some truth was retold by the Rev E A Bray: the church 'was erected by a wealthy merchant who vowed, in the midst of a tremendous storm at sea, possibly addressing himself to his patron St Michael, that if he escaped in safety he would build a church on the first land he descried'. Giffard was a landowner rather than a merchant, and although the tor can be seen from the sea, it is 17 miles from the coast and thus unlikely to be the first land to catch the eye, unless all the countryside beneath was obscured under a thick blanket of fog.

It's a cheery little story, though the fact that exactly the same one is repeated for a couple of other churches in the southwest does not count in its favour.

The other two prominent legends have the Devil interfering with the work of building the church until defeated by the church's patron saint.

At 37ft by 14ft 6in, the church is one of Britain's smallest parish churches (the smallest is reckoned to be St Beuno's, p26, in Somerset). The low walls are 3ft thick and made of the tor's own volcanic rock, dressed with locally quarried green slate stone.

The dedication to St Michael is common among churches found in high places, on account of the heights traditionally inhabited by angels, who count the saint as their captain. It was given to Tavistock Abbey, whose monks established an annual Michaelmas fair that ran for over 300 years in its precincts until around 1550. In 1319, the brothers also took it upon themselves to rebuild the church as a chapelry in order that it might serve the local district. That same year it was consecrated by Bishop Stapeldon, a man who was to wind up lynched by the mob in London while looking after the kingdom for an absent Edward II.

Given the highly exposed nature of the summit, it is unsurprising to learn that there are plans afoot to replace the roof, which itself only goes back to Victorian days and is very flat-pitched. When an examination of the roof beams took place, an unexpected discovery was made: graffiti from the times of both world wars.

Men had carved their names into the wood prior to going off to fight, presumably in a bid to leave something of themselves behind in case they never returned. Most of the names date from 1916–18 or 1943–55 and some are written in flawless copperplate font.

There are now five bells hung in the tower but for centuries the church got by on two or three. One of these was cast in the 14th or 15th century and was inscribed in Latin, *Gallus vocor ego, solus per omne sono*: 'I am called the cock, and I alone sound above all.'

The interior of the church is pleasantly shadowy and sombre. Unlike the solidly medieval exterior, it is almost entirely very late Victorian, dating from the Bedford restoration. A notable exception is the plain octagonal granite font. The most striking window is a modern depiction of St Michael by Bideford artist James Paterson, spreading over three lights.

The view from St Michael's is one of the finest from any church in Britain. On fine days, Exmoor is visible 40 miles northeast; Bodmin Moor's Brown Willy, Cornwall's highest point, is to the west; and south is Whitsand Bay and Plymouth Sound (sailors on their way to Plymouth used St Michael's as a landmark).

Finally, if you attend the marvellously atmospheric Christmas Day carol service and there's snow about, do take your sledge. By tradition, after the service, congregants slide back down the tor.

3 ST BEUNO'S
CULBONE

It's all but impossible to look upon this church in its woodland setting and not fall for it instantly.

SPIRITUAL ORIENTATION
Church of England

PHYSICAL ORIENTATION
Culbone, Porlock Weir, Minehead, Somerset TA24 8PQ
Grid reference: SS 842 482
OS Landranger map 181

PUBLIC TRANSPORT
Getting to St Beuno's requires walking boots and determination. Arrive in style in Minehead on the steam railway (westsomersetrailway. vticket.co.uk; 01643 704996) then walk the short distance to Bancks Street to catch the no. 10 bus (webberbus.com; 0800 0963039) to the Ship Inn at Porlock Weir. From here follow the South West Coast Path westwards for just over a mile until you reach the church.

OPENING ARRANGEMENTS
Always open.

SERVICES
11am 1st Sunday (Holy Communion)
3pm 3rd Sunday (Evensong)
Occasionally, changes are made to this schedule. For details contact Rev Colin Burke (01598 741270).

here is no road to St Beuno's. Visitors must walk a section of the South West Coast Path up to a wooded hollow a quarter of a mile from the sea and 400ft above the waves. There was once a small settlement in this remote Exmoor dell – a group of cottages and shacks in which dwelt charcoal burners and others who scratched a living in the woods. Now there's just a single house. It's said that Culbone was once also home to a leper colony and that's not hard to imagine because there's something about the place that suggests that just about anything could have happened here in the tenebrous light beneath the trees.

The church that bore witness to the life and death of the village is a delight to behold. Best viewed when approached from the west, it looks perfectly at home in its sylvan setting and, at only 35ft by 12ft, it is said to be the smallest complete parish church in Britain. Given that, you might expect it to be a simple affair – perhaps a nave and nothing much else. St Beuno's, however, also runs to a chancel, a porch and a spire, or something approaching a spire. Such dainty dimensions somewhat limit the size of the parish it can serve – as the church's own leaflet notes, there is 'seating (in some discomfort) for 33 people'. It's as well then

that the district is all but depopulated. Indeed, it's impressive that there are enough people around whose faith compels them to make the trek into the woods every fortnight to keep the church in service.

The age of St Beuno's (pronounced 'Bayno') is unclear, though there are parts that are discernibly pre-Norman, evidence backed up by the church's appearance in the Domesday Book. However, to declare it to be of any particular age would be invidious because it is such a mish-mash of additions and reworkings from various centuries that it is nothing short of miraculous that the end result is so aesthetically pleasing.

The walls of the nave are made of rubble and are mostly 12th century. The red sandstone porch comes from the 13th century, while the roof dates from the 15th. The lovely little two-light window in the north wall of the sanctuary is fashioned from a single block of sandstone and is from at least Norman times (the dating Pevsner goes for) but could even be Saxon. Look at it from the outside and you'll notice a face in bas-relief. Is it that of a leopard? It certainly looks like one. Meanwhile, the chancel's east wall is a late 19th-century repair job. The unusual wagon roof was added to the chancel at the same time, presumably to complement the nave's wagon roof, which harks back to the 15th century. The spire, made of deal and slate and so short it's barely worthy of the name, was added around 1810. (The story goes that it was the top of the spire from Porlock Church which blew off and was transported to Culbone. There's no truth in this.)

The pair of tiny bells hung on high and the cross in the churchyard continue this theme. The bells date from the 17th and the 14th century respectively (apparently making the latter the oldest bell in west Somerset, a fact to set the heart aflutter). The base of the cross was carved in the 15th century while the cross itself was the design of H M Drury in 1966. Given all this zipping about from century to century, you almost expect some of the gravestones to be dated in the future. Two interesting surnames crop up on them: Red and Axe. The former is found inside the church as well, though in rather unfortunate circumstances. The name of churchwarden Nicholas Red is on a board directly beneath the Ten Commandments, as though he himself had given them.

It's difficult to pass through the (14th-century) doorway and not immediately people the church with characters from *Lorna Doone*, though it's St Beuno's sister church, St Mary's at Oare, that is more closely associated with R D Blackmore's novel. Those people, as the church leaflet suggests, might have found themselves somewhat cramped, partly because the enormously thick walls make the church a sort of anti-Tardis, a place even smaller on the inside than it looks on the outside. The seating includes a sturdy Jacobean box pew, reserved for the Lovelace family. It has outlived the hall, Ashley Combe House, in which they lived.

The font is yet another hybrid: a wonderful eggcup that is either Norman or Saxon set on a stone step that is Victorian. Also worth looking out for are the two Green Men in the ceiling of the chancel, a glass angel behind the altar that appears to be missing its Christmas tree, and a wonderful old (and somewhat dusty) harmonium standing by to prod the congregation into hymnody.

But what of the curious-sounding saint who gave his name to the church and the lost village (Culbone is a corruption of 'Kil Beun', meaning 'Church of St Beuno')? He was born in Wales in the late 6th century and became an important abbot. However, the popular story that he brought his niece St Winefride back from the dead after she had been beheaded is, sadly, a fable. It's appropriate then that his church also appears to have sprung from a fairytale. 🪶

4 ST EDWOLD'S
STOCKWOOD

The rather artless bell-cote is apt to charm the visitor, even from afar.

SPIRITUAL ORIENTATION
Church of England (Churches Conservation Trust)

PHYSICAL ORIENTATION
By Church Farm, Stockwood, Dorset DT2 0NG
Grid reference: ST 590 069
OS Landranger map 194

PUBLIC TRANSPORT
From Chetnole railway station (gwr.com; 0345 7000125), a request stop, turn right and walk a little under a mile.

OPENING ARRANGEMENTS
Open daily.

SERVICES
Two a year. Evening Prayer is held on St Edwold's Day (29 August) at 5pm; and a Carol Service takes place in the week before Christmas. Contact Janet Danks for details (01935 83757; jandjdanks@tiscali.co.uk).

ntil the opening in 2014 of a little hermitage dedicated to St Edwold at the Franciscan Friary at Hilfield in Dorset, there was apparently no other St Edwold's church anywhere in the world but in Stockwood. This is perhaps less surprising when you consider that St Edwold is something of an obscure saint. You will search in vain for a biography that delivers more than sketchy details or even a second paragraph about him. *The Penguin Dictionary of Saints* doesn't even give him a namecheck.

It doesn't help that he was not even the only saint in his family. His older brother St Edmund found greater fame as the East Anglian king who was captured by the Danes after a battle at Thetford in 869 and executed, reportedly by being tied to a tree and shot through with arrows, then beheaded. As a consequence Edwold was asked by the East Angles to take his brother's place on the throne. Perhaps understandably he declared himself less than keen. He left East Anglia 'hating the world because hard fortune took him and his brother'. The next time anything is heard of him he is in Cerne in Dorset, home to the famous chalk giant. Edwold apparently established himself as

a hermit next to a spring called the Silver Well, a place said to have been visited two centuries earlier by St Augustine.

Although his Perpendicular-style church in Stockwood is not near a spring, it is at least by a small stream. After passing down a track and crossing part of a field, visitors negotiate this waterway by means of a small brick footbridge – the same place the worshippers would have crossed in the 15th century when the present building was constructed.

Today, St Edwold's appears to have been dropped into a back garden. At just 30ft by 12ft, it's one of the smallest complete churches in England and its proximity to the farmhouse that overlooks it only serves to emphasise its diminutive character. The very fact that it was

dedicated to St Edwold suggests that an earlier church, probably pre-Norman, once stood here. Indeed, the name Stockwood comes from Stoke St Edwold, so it's possible that the man himself spent some time in the district.

The first thing you notice on approaching the church is the rather wonderful bell-cote at the western end. It looks not unlike a maharajah's crown with its four little columns capped by a dome. On top of this is a ball and four pinnacles of stone where the precious jewels of the headpiece might be. Below it is a porch added in 1636 – the keystone of the doorway's arch helpfully recording the year. The opposite end of the church has a generous trefoiled three-light window which helps make it surprisingly bright inside for a building hemmed in by foliage and brick.

The one oddity of the exterior can be found in the south wall between the two windows. Here, set into the stones and turned on its side, is a medieval piscina. It once graced the inside of the church and would have been an integral part of the preparations for the mass. This bizarre re-imagining of a standard church fixture probably took place during a so-called restoration that occurred at some point after 1870. In that year, a Mrs Susannah Strangways Horner reported that the church was 'neatly pewed'. Those pews, along with the rest of the church furniture, were removed in the restoration, which doubtless also accounts for the presence of the somewhat dull font and the clunky altar rails.

The unfortunate plundering of the church means that its most striking element is now an entirely modern addition. A colourful icon of a magnificently blue-eyed St Edwold depicts him holding his one and only church in his left hand. The fact that the artist has been left with so little in the way of motifs with which to illustrate his life – there are some coins, a well, and a (rather delightful-looking) hermitage, bulked out with a hand of blessing extending from a heavenly cloud – lends the painting an inescapable air of pathos. The icon sits on a low table in a corner beside the altar. Sadly, with no village as such to sustain it, the church Edwold cradles so jealously was declared redundant in 1959.

The saint was considered 'an heremite of high perfection' (we won't quibble about the fact that you can't really have degrees of perfection). He did not have to maintain this dizzying level of holiness for long, dying as he did a year after arriving in Dorset. When the monastery at Cerne was rebuilt, he was reburied in the choir of the new abbey, an act that demonstrates the high esteem in which he was once held.

St Edwold's Day falls on 29 August, so if you are planning a summer-time visit to the church, it might be apposite to arrive on that day, if only to let the troubled saint know that he's not completely forgotten. 🦡

ST LAURENCE'S
BRADFORD-ON-AVON

A visit here provides a rare opportunity to appreciate Saxon architecture in its purest form, unsullied by later improvements.

SPIRITUAL ORIENTATION
Church of England/ Ecumenical

PHYSICAL ORIENTATION
Church Street, Bradford-on-Avon, Wiltshire BA15 1LW
Grid reference: ST 824 609
OS Landranger map 173

PUBLIC TRANSPORT
The church is within easy walking distance of Bradford-on-Avon railway station (gwr.com; 0345 7000125). A handy footbridge connects the southern bank of the Avon with Church Street.

OPENING ARRANGEMENTS
2.30–4.30pm daily from April to September
Guided tours for groups can be arranged by contacting the churchwardens Trevor Ford (01225 862240) or Judith Holland (01225 866215).

SERVICES
6pm 1st Sunday, June to September (Compline)
6pm 4th Sunday, June to September (Evensong)
Noon every Friday, June to September (Eucharist)
Noon every Thursday (Sabeel – prayer for peace in the Middle East)
Occasional Lutheran, Roman Catholic and Greek Orthodox services.

here's many a church that has disappeared because it has simply crumbled away or been demolished. By contrast, there are very few that stay right where they are yet contrive to go missing for hundreds of years, in the middle of a town. But that's exactly what happened to the church of St Laurence.

There's some debate about when the church was built. An observation made by the 12th-century historian William of Malmesbury supports the theory that it was established as early as 705 by St Aldhelm. However, the architectural style posits a much later date: the early 11th century. Of course, it might be that a church was originally founded on this spot in the early 8th century and built upon later. Alternatively, St Aldhelm may have established a place of worship on the site of the current Holy Trinity church that stands opposite. There is one thing we can say with certainty, though: St Laurence's is Saxon.

Once you've slipped through the doorway from the porticus to the nave there's an overwhelming sense of being somewhere thoroughly ancient. With no electric lighting, and only a few narrow windows to let in the sunshine, your eyes take a second or two to adjust. The ceiling is also remarkably high for such a small building – if it didn't feel like sacrilege, it might be described as like walking into a huge wardrobe or, in winter, perhaps a huge fridge.

Furnished with just five wooden chairs, a rail, and a couple of candelabra hanging from the ceiling, there's an austerity to the place that puts you immediately in mind of monks.

'Remember your vow of poverty,' it breathes. This message is undercut somewhat by the breathtaking beauty of the place – derived in no small part from the simplicity of its design and the boldness of its proportions – which renders any visitor rich.

We can count ourselves fortunate that the Normans preferred to use the much larger Holy Trinity church, because their lack of enthusiasm for St Laurence's led to it being abandoned. It thus arrived in the

21st century unaltered, which makes it exceedingly rare for a Saxon church in Britain (see also Odda's Chapel, p139).

That's not to say it hasn't had an interesting journey. By 1715 we know it was being used as a school, while the chancel became a cottage, the church's high ceiling accommodating three storeys. It also served time as a warehouse. With a schoolmaster's house leaning against the south wall – perhaps where a second porticus once existed – and other buildings crowding round it, the fact that this was ever a church was simply forgotten and St Laurence's disappeared.

It took a local vicar, Canon Jones, to haul the church back from the void into which it had vanished. An avid historian, when two Saxon carved angels were found during repairs to the building in 1857, he set about investigating. Climbing up the steep slope above Holy Trinity, Jones looked down on the jumble of roofs below and made out the shape of a Saxon church. St Laurence's was discovered.

In 1871, the canon came across a throwaway line in William of Malmesbury's 1125 work *Gesta Pontificum Anglorum*: 'To this day at that place there exists a little church which Aldhem [sic] is said to have built to the name of the most blessed Laurence.' The church was duly reconsecrated and reopened for worship.

Restored to its original function, it sits in relative isolation today, in a little patch of lawn, its honey-coloured stone once

again glowing in the sunlight. It's really in remarkably good condition – only the west wall had to be rebuilt and the Victorian artisans who did it made a fine job of matching it to the rest of the building. High up and circling the building there is also an eye-catching blind arcade (so called because all the arches are filled in).

The entrance nowadays is via the north porticus. The window here is original, as are those in the south wall of the nave and chancel – all of which are very small by modern standards, window panes being a luxury often beyond the budget of even the wealthier echelons of Saxon society. If one of the drivers for the building of the church was to provide a resting place for the bones of Edward the Martyr, brother of Æthelred, this sombre lighting would have been most fitting.

The plainness of the nave draws the eye to the narrow portal topped with a Romanesque arch that provides the only opening between the nave and the chancel. This stark separation serves to make the church feel even smaller than it is. It also adds a dash of real drama, for the doorway affords only the merest glimpse of the chancel. The sun's rays, streaming through an unseen window, illuminate the east wall like a spotlight.

Against that wall is the solid rectangular mass of an altar created from Saxon stones found in the vicinity. Above it is a ring of Doulting stone carved by

John Maine RA in 2012. The artist has attached it to the wall, placing beneath it a piece of fossilised tree 150 million years old and a fragment from a Celtic cross. To be honest, it is not immediately obvious that the three pieces form a work of art – against the patchwork of ashlar they simply look right, as if they've always been there.

Before you leave, take a moment to look up high on the east wall of the nave. There you'll see the carvings of heavenly figures whose unearthing led to the rediscovery of the church – St Laurence's very own guardian angels. 🪶

BREMILHAM CHURCH
NEAR MALMESBURY

Who would have imagined that Britain's smallest church would find room in its bijou nave for such a colossal bell?

SPIRITUAL ORIENTATION
Church of England

PHYSICAL ORIENTATION
Cowage Farm, Foxley, Malmesbury, Wiltshire
SN16 0JJ
Grid reference: ST 903 860
OS Landranger map 173

PUBLIC TRANSPORT
From Chippenham railway station (gwr.com; 0345 7000125) take the 92 bus (coachstyleltd-wiltshire. co.uk; 01249 782224) to Malmesbury. The chapel is about 2 miles from Malmesbury and can be reached by taking the Foxley road across the River Avon and southwest out of town. Sadly, there are no bus services along that route. Take the turning off the road on the right at the Cowage Farm Business Units sign.

OPENING ARRANGEMENTS
Always open, but it is suggested that visitors call Mrs Collins (01666 823173) beforehand.

SERVICES
Once a year, on Rogation Sunday (the Sunday before Ascension Day), which usually falls in May.

here is a certain trainspotter-esque thrill in spending time in what is Britain's smallest active church. Active, in this case, is perhaps overstating things a little – there's just a single service a year – meaning that the smallest properly active church is St Trillo's Chapel in Rhos-on-Sea (p251). However, there's no denying its smallness: the church is just 13ft by 11ft and is topped by a low gabled roof. As others before have observed, the building bears an uncanny resemblance to a house from the board game Monopoly. Understandably, the 50 or so people who turn up for the annual

service on Rogation Sunday are obliged to spend it seated on the handkerchief-sized patch of grass in front of the church, whatever the weather.

Not content with attracting a certain notoriety on account of its size, the chapel's location is also very peculiar: it's in a farmyard, many of whose buildings are now business units, one of which is a tanning salon.

It must be said that such frenetic activity is not what the local parish is used to. It's one of the smallest and least populated parishes in Wiltshire, and from the 16th century onwards Cowage has

been the only farm within its borders. Bremilham struggled on until the 1980s before finally being subsumed into the next-door parish of Foxley. It means that any Rogationtide procession in which the beating of the old parish bounds takes place is not altogether taxing, particularly as the terrain is also mainly flat.

Such a dearth of potential parishioners might seem to explain the diminutive character of the church. However, what can be seen today is a relatively modern mortuary chapel. The church that stood here for many centuries was actually about three times the size. The precise date of the original building is unclear but we do know that Amesbury Priory was granted the tithes that came into the church in 1179 and it's assumed that it was built a short time before this.

Hemmed in by the Avon to the north and one of that river's many tributaries to the south, the church saw out its life in quiet obscurity, passing through the hands of one lord of the manor after another. The road near which it stands used to carry the Oxford to Bristol traffic, but a turnpiked thoroughfare created in 1756 a little to the north condemned the church to the shadows once more.

At least the 18th century proved more exciting than most. In 1715, the church was inherited by Philip, Duke of Wharton. He was a Jacobite, an alcoholic, the founder of the original Hellfire Club and, according to Alexander Pope, a man 'too rash for thought, for action too refined'. His estate, including the church, was confiscated in 1729 after he was convicted of treason for proving Pope wrong by fighting with the Jacobites against the English in Spain.

A few decades later, Daniel Freer, the Bremilham rector from 1760 to 1793, 'was described to the bishop as a madman' – not always the epithet you want to hear applied to your rector, particularly as, in this case, it appears to have been justified. At least he wasn't around much to annoy the few Bremilham locals. He lived out at Westport and somehow contrived to celebrate Communion at the church on just one occasion in the first 23 years of his tenure.

Like Freer, the church was never dedicated. It was reported in 1731 to have consisted of a 25ft by 13ft nave and a 13ft by 11ft chancel. Come 1809, we also hear of the existence of a wooden bell-cote, as well as two 13th-century lancet windows and other windows of 16th-century origin. By 1874, however, the decision had been taken to demolish the church and replace it with a much smaller mortuary chapel the size of the former church's chancel. To compound this felony, Bremilham's only bell was taken off and hung in Foxley church. In return it received Foxley's bell, which was cracked. It still sits on the floor at Bremilham, complete with its headstock

and frame, as if the little church had space to burn.

As might be expected, there is not a great deal inside aside from the bell – not even an altar. Four chairs line the wall, a small organ stands beneath a window, while a cross and two candlesticks perch on a windowsill. The main focus of the cramped room is an item that is often of secondary importance in a church: the font. It is octagonal, in the Perpendicular style, and adorned with quatrefoils. Although the creamy stone is somewhat damaged and incised, it lends the church a certain dignity.

It is a dignity Bremilham has not always enjoyed, even in its comparatively short life. By the 1980s, it was being used as a turkey house. Thankfully, when Kenneth and Bindy Collins bought Cowage Farm they cleaned the chapel up, asked a bishop to come and bless it, and opened it up as a place of worship again.

A simple headstone marks the spot in front of the church where Kenneth Collins is now buried. It was the first interment in the churchyard for exactly a hundred years, and the building's original purpose as a mortuary chapel was once again fulfilled.

ST LAWRENCE OLD CHURCH

ST LAWRENCE

The cocooned feeling you get while inside is rather like exploring a chalky cavern.

SPIRITUAL ORIENTATION

Church of England

PHYSICAL ORIENTATION

Seven Sisters Road,
St Lawrence, Isle of Wight,
Hampshire PO38 1UY
Grid reference: SZ 536 766
OS Landranger map 196

PUBLIC TRANSPORT

From Shanklin railway
station (southwesttrains.co.
uk; 0345 6000650), walk to
the bus station and take a
no. 3 bus to Albert Street in
Ventnor, where you should
change to a no. 6 bus (both
islandbuses.info; 01983
827000), alighting on
Whitwell Road near
St Lawrence Shute. It's less
than 0.5 miles to the church,
walking up St Lawrence
Shute and left along Seven
Sisters Road.

OPENING ARRANGEMENTS

Open daily between about
9am and 4pm.

SERVICES

5.30pm 1st Sunday (Said
Communion)
6pm 1st Sunday (Evensong)
– directly following on from
the Communion service
This schedule is subject to
change. Check details with
Rev Dr Nigel Porter (01983
731922).

 Lawrence Old Church is almost certainly a record holder. At a mere 25ft by 11ft and with a very low roof, for many hundreds of years it was probably the smallest parish church in Britain. Only as recently as 1842 was a chancel added (probably by Lord Yarborough) and the claim to that title passed to St Beuno's (p26) in Somerset. However, that church is 10ft longer than the original St Lawrence's, so the plucky little (at 40ft long it is still very little indeed) place of worship on the south coast of the Isle of Wight clings to its proud boast of being the longest serving smallest parish church in the land.

St Lawrence is a village with not one eponymous church, but two, hence the need to refer to this one as St Lawrence Old Church. The very compactness that lies at the heart of the venerable building's charm also proved its undoing. As the village grew in the early 19th century, the church, which can seat about 40 people, could not cope with the burgeoning congregation and a decision was taken to build something more substantial further down the hill. George Gilbert Scott, a Gothic Revivalist and one of the pre-eminent architects of his day, was duly commissioned and in 1876 the new St Lawrence's church opened its doors, consigning the old church to the supporting role it has played ever since.

This first St Lawrence's dates from the 12th century, and was almost certainly built as a chapel to a nearby Saxon manor house that has since disappeared. The dedication is to a 3rd-century Roman martyr traditionally said to have been roasted on a grid iron (he was probably beheaded) and suggests that St Lawrence was in all likelihood the manorial family's own patron saint. By degrees the chapel assumed the part of a parish church, saving the local populace the inconvenience of walking further afield to take Mass or bury their loved ones.

An extract from Worsley's *The History of the Isle of Wight* (1781) is available in the church and tells part of the story of St Lawrence's by means of a series of engravings that have provided valuable clues to its development. A 1781 work shows the church kitted out with a stone belfry but no porch. Fourteen years later, a print in a publication called *A Tour to the Isle of Wight* by Charles Tomkins gives the church a wooden spire masking the belfry. In 1805 a porch has appeared and by 1827 the wooden spire has come down, never to be seen again. The 1842 expansion, captured 13 years after the event, shows the chancel windows framed by an attractive stucco dressing.

A friendly sign at the entrance to the grounds tempts weary walkers inside with promises of cold drinks and biscuits. Any footsore travellers must first pass through a very small graveyard, which, over the centuries, has very visibly expanded westward, bursting through wall and hedge as each plot of land filled up with locals who had gone to meet their Maker.

Once inside the snug confines of the little church, there is plenty of interest to see. The old font was snaffled by the new church but the piscina in the south wall is 13th century and a stoup (for holy water) probably dates from the 15th. The nave is flanked by two long rows of wooden Georgian hat pegs, while on the chancel arch stands a rather fetching statuette of St Lawrence. He is shown holding a grid iron that is reassuringly far too small for him to have been martyred upon. By the

refreshment table you'll find the old north entrance to the church, which has long since been blocked up.

There is also a little mystery to wonder at. The windows in the nave were put in at different times and are at a rare old jumble of heights. The most intriguing of these is the large window in the north wall, which is very low indeed. There was clearly a reason for this at the time but its purpose can now only be guessed at.

While you're in the village, do visit the church's 19th-century namesake. It boasts an array of Pre-Raphaelite stained-glass windows by Edward Burne-Jones, William Morris and Ford Madox Brown.

However, before you leave old St Lawrence's, take a moment to read a poem called *The Little Hatpeg Church* by 'M. J. T.' which is posted up in the porch. It's no *Gray's Elegy* but the final lines do at least possess the satisfying tang of Arnold's *Dover Beach*. That's more than can be said for the two-part poem from the mid-1800s on view alongside it. It was composed, if one might abuse that word for a moment, by the parish clerk, a man who was evidently in thrall to the towering poetic genius of William McGonagall. It appears to do us the favour of fixing the date of the church at 1197. However, the fact that that allows the poet to pair it with the immortal line ''Twas built that we may know the way to heaven' does cast a shadow of suspicion over the assertion. 🪶

ST SWITHUN-UPON-KINGSGATE

WINCHESTER

It's quite special to be on top of a medieval city gate, but being in a rare surviving medieval city gate church adds even more lustre.

SPIRITUAL ORIENTATION

Church of England

PHYSICAL ORIENTATION

St Swithun Street, Winchester, Hampshire SO23 9JP
Grid reference: SU 481 290
OS Landranger map 185

PUBLIC TRANSPORT

From Winchester railway station (southwesttrains.co.uk; 0345 6000650) it's less than a mile to the church. The most pleasant route is to follow signs to the cathedral, pass the entrance and bear left towards the deanery. Walk to the left of the deanery and around the back onto St Swithun Street and the church is almost immediately to your left.

OPENING ARRANGEMENTS

Open daily 9.30am–5pm (or dusk if earlier).

SERVICES

Alternates each Sunday between 9.30am (Holy Communion) and 6pm (Evensong)
Call the parish office for details (01962 849434; threesaints.org.uk).

 place of surprising quietude in the heart of throbbing Winchester, St Swithun-upon-Kingsgate has provided sanctuary from the madding crowd for over 750 years. A single narrow room, it calls to mind the hiding place of the disciples after the death of Jesus. When St Swithun's was built, however, it would have been far from hidden away, sitting as it does on top of one of the medieval gates into the city. Placing a church on top of a city gate was quite common in the Middle Ages but St Swithun's is a rare survivor.

It's unfortunate then that the first record we have of its existence comes from a 1264 report detailing its burning down by angry citizens during a dispute with the local priory. It was rebuilt, becoming a parish church in 1539 when the monastery at Winchester was dissolved by Henry VIII, only to find itself in a state of decrepitude by the 17th century. Indeed, at that time we find the gate porter and his family living in the church and that his wife 'doth keep swine at ye ende of the Chapell' – the swine presumably referring to pigs rather than her husband. At some point after 1660, the building was repaired and restored to its original function and has never again been at such a low ebb.

The saint to whom the church is dedicated was a local lad who went on to become Bishop of Winchester in 852. It is believed that before he died, 10 years later, he was a tutor to the young Alfred, later Alfred the Great, founder of the British Navy and burner of cakes. However, Swithun is rather better known for his powers as a weather forecaster:

St Swithun's Day, if then dost rain
For forty days it will remain:
St Swithun's Day, if then be fair
For forty days 'twill rain nae mair.

The rhyme apparently has its basis in the storm that is said to have broken over Winchester on the day his relics were transferred to a shrine inside the cathedral. The tempest was Swithun's way of showing his dismay at being moved, since on his deathbed he had asked to be buried by the door of Winchester Cathedral where parishioners would be obliged to walk over him.

Before climbing the covered staircase up to the church, look at the battlements on the south wall – a reminder that, though a holy building, this was still part of a defensive structure. The walls are filled with rubble, covered with flint and are very thick. The roof, meanwhile, is steeply pitched and topped with rich red tiles. The dormer windows on its south side were installed in the 19th century to admit more light. Disappointingly, the stairs themselves only go back to 1954 but the timber framework is from about 1500.

Once upon a time, the inside of the church was painted with murals and

adorned with statues in its three niches. An examination of the walls in 1953 revealed no fewer than three layers of paintings, though none in a good enough state to preserve. The earliest paintings dated from the late 15th or early 16th century but were apparently eradicated by zealous soldiers of the Reformation. More zealots, though this time of the Puritan ilk, removed the statues from the niches (one of St Swithun probably stood in the east wall beside the altar) and obliterated the niches themselves to prevent new idolatry taking place.

Though none of the medieval stained glass has survived, the east window is worth inspecting. It was transferred here in 1961 from the Church of St Peter's (now a theatre) in nearby Chesil Street and replaced a rather poor-quality Victorian window. The sections are thought to be part of a depiction of the Annunciation. Meanwhile, although St Swithun's statue may be gone, he is represented in the south window, which is very late Victorian. The bridge he was believed to have built over the River Itchen is shown beneath his feet. Alongside him is St Ethelwold, a scholar, founder of monasteries and tireless reformer who was not known to suffer fools gladly.

The church furniture is mainly modern or late Victorian. The lectern, prayer desk and chair are all from 1899, as is the cardinal chair, though this has the distinction of having come, in all likelihood, from Burma. The pews are of oak and many were built by a parishioner called Colin Campbell in 1968. The spellings of the verse from Psalms inscribed on the altar rail immediately give it away as being from a more distant period: 'I will wash my handes in innocency soe will I compasse Thy altar O Lord.' The rail was brought to the church in 1960 from a nearby preparatory school and is from the 17th century.

This splash of antiquity came far too late to be seen by the great English novelist Anthony Trollope, though presumably he visited at some point because the church (thinly disguised as St Cuthbert's) features in his tale *The Warden*:

The Church is a singular little Gothic building, perched over a gateway, through which the Close is entered, and is approached by a flight of stone steps which leads down under the archway of a gate. It is no bigger than an ordinary room – perhaps twenty seven feet long by eighteen wide – but still it is a perfect church...

In the shadow of the famous cathedral, tucked away in a side street, this 'perfect church' is often overlooked. This means there are rarely hordes of visitors and St Swithun's remains a quiet haven of spirituality in a noisy, rapacious world.

OLD CHURCH OF ST MARY THE VIRGIN
PRESTON CANDOVER

The Victorian prolixity and heraldic sensibilities of the unusual painted glass window combine to create something rather striking.

SPIRITUAL ORIENTATION

Formerly Church of England (Churches Conservation Trust)

PHYSICAL ORIENTATION

Preston Candover, Basingstoke, Hampshire RG25 2EN

Grid reference: SU 603 414
OS Landranger map 185

PUBLIC TRANSPORT

From Basingstoke railway station (gwr.com; 0345 7000125) walk the short distance to the bus station and take the C41 bus (stagecoachbus.com; 0345 1210190) to the Purefoy

Arms in Preston Candover. The church is just off the main road to the south of the pub.

OPENING ARRANGEMENTS

Open daily.

SERVICES

None.

In terms of cubic capacity, there surely cannot be another church in all of England that contains so much to interest the visitor as does the Old Church of St Mary the Virgin. This will come as a surprise to anyone who knows their Pevsner and has read his terse four-word review of the place: 'In it one lancet.' One can only surmise that he got out of bed on the wrong side the day he paid a call.

Admittedly, at first sight the fragment of the late 12th-century rubble-and-flint church that has been left to us is not much to look at. The nave and chapel, which by all accounts were rather delightful, suffered demolition in 1884, leaving just the chancel standing. However, this lends the church a certain vulnerability that is wont to soften the heart of those who look upon it. Frankly, it did extremely well to survive intact as long as it did. The church caught fire in 1683 and underwent restorations in both 1796 and 1852 to save it from dereliction.

The decision to build a new place of worship in Preston Candover (a church that was also named after the Virgin Mary, which explains the older church's retronym) throws an interesting light on church practice at the time. The Incorporated Church Building Society was willing to make a grant for its construction because all the seating was to be made free. In the old church, 60 per cent of the seats were privately rented, which merely bolstered the financial apartheid that existed in society at large.

Unusually, the churchyard boasts both yews and ewes, the latter keeping the grass down so efficiently that you wonder why it's not a sight seen more often around churches. William Buckley lies here, resting from his twin feats of building Moundsmere Manor and creating the very first herd of cows to be tested for tuberculosis. There are also two very obvious sarsen stones that are said to mark the extent of the original building.

The priest's personal doorway in the south wall has been blocked up, but towards the bottom of the left door jamb you'll find a mass dial, a medieval device designed to show parishioners the time of the next service.

As you enter St Mary's, take a moment to consider the plight of the Rev Humphry Humphrys. In life, he had to put up with all the inevitable jokes about his name. In death he finds himself buried slap bang in the doorway of the church he served for 30 years as a curate, meaning that parishioners literally walk all over him. (It's possible, of course, that this is what he requested – à la St Swithun (p48) and Lawrence le Leche (p163, Steetley Chapel), in which case, spare your pity.)

The wall you pass through was once the open arch of the chancel and was built after the rest of the church was torn down. If you examine the doorway you'll notice that it incorporates lots of unmatched carved stones that were presumably salvaged from the demolished nave and chapel. The other three walls are 13th century in origin. Close the door behind

you and there's a sense of having walked into a cupboard. Quite a cluttered cupboard at that. For a start, it contains not just one but two biers, one on top of the other. The upper one probably dates from the 18th century while the lower one is later but provides quite a spectacle with its four bicycle wheels and Victorian-looking suspension. The biers' presence here is a reminder that the chancel itself was saved from demolition in 1884 so that it could be used as a mortuary chapel.

Behind them, in the north wall, is Pevsner's lancet. This narrow window is late 12th century and as such is the church's earliest dateable feature. It is,

however, rather put in the shade by the church's largest and most modern window, installed in 1892.

When it comes to the decorative arts, with the notable exceptions of the Arts and Crafts and Pre-Raphaelite Movements, the Victorians tend to get a bad press, and perhaps deservedly so. However, though it may not be to everyone's taste, there's something unarguably impressive about the window in the east wall. Eschewing clichéd or mawkish representations of Christ or a saint – the temptation to revisit a scene from the life of the Virgin Mary cannot have been insignificant – the artist (or whoever commissioned the artist) has

opted for diagonal stripes of Gothic script with virtually the only colour coming from a band of glass that frames the piece.

The text itself could do with a good editor to sharpen it up but the overall effect is really quite something. It's as if someone has put a design from the Knights of the Round Table onto a Newcastle United shirt and slanted it. Or perhaps its contemporary look is down to our familiarity with the ubiquitous bar code – you be the judge.

On the same wall there are two mysterious-looking painted circles, each with a cross inside it – the sort of thing thriller writer Dan Brown would have based an entire trilogy around. These are consecration crosses, painted on the spots the bishop anointed with holy oil when he consecrated the church. These particular crosses date from the 13th century when St Mary's was reconsecrated.

Both the altar table and font have been lost to the new St Mary's. The piece of furniture that remains is something of a Frankenstein's monster. It resembles a low lectern but is actually a prayer desk cobbled together from various other fixtures and fittings, notably the former screen. The communion rail from the old church now graces the east wall, while the sections of panelling previously saw service as box pews.

Beneath your feet are 32 re-used medieval tiles bearing a range of designs. Half of them have been very fetchingly arranged in a square set at an angle. Also on the floor is the impressive brass dedicated to Katharine Dabrigecort, who died on 6 June 1607.

More interesting historically though is the memorial to Elizabeth Soper, which confusingly refers to the year '1733/4'. The ambiguity of the date is explained by John E Vigar in his excellent guide to the church:

The country was in the limbo state of recognising both the Julian and Gregorian calendars, whose years started on different dates. In England, dates before 1752 were usually calculated according to the Julian calendar, but as most of continental Europe used the Gregorian calendar, dates that occurred in the 'overlap' months of January, February and March (up to the 25th, which was New Year's Day in the Julian calendar) were often written like this to reflect both.

Sir Nikolaus Pevsner died in 1983. Though St Mary's saw little use as a mortuary chapel it did manage to see the great man out, remaining in service until the following year. If stones can feel emotion, this must have given it no little satisfaction. 🦋

ST HUBERT'S
IDSWORTH

This solitary church boasts an astonishingly complete 14th-century fresco featuring John the Baptist and, possibly, a werewolf.

SPIRITUAL ORIENTATION
Church of England

PHYSICAL ORIENTATION
Finchdean, Idsworth, Waterlooville, Hampshire PO8 0BA
Grid reference: SU 742 140
OS Landranger map 197

PUBLIC TRANSPORT
Take a train to Rowlands Castle (southwesttrains.co.uk; 0345 6000650) then it's a 2.5-mile walk or cycle ride following the railway line north through Finchdean and onwards until the church shows itself in an open field on the right-hand side. There are no buses along this route.

OPENING ARRANGEMENTS
Normally open daily from 9am to dusk.

SERVICES
9.30am Sunday (Matins, Communion or Family Service)
9am Friday (Morning Prayer).

 here's something pleasingly anachronistic about a church that stands all alone in the middle of an arable field. 'Something here,' you muse sagely to yourself, reaching for your deerstalker and meerschaum pipe, 'is amiss.' In the case of St Hubert's, what's amiss is a missing village, that of Idsworth. The church is nearly all that remains and, as you climb up a lavishly wide greenway through fields of crops to make its acquaintance, you'll be trampling over the bones of a Saxon village that disappeared nigh on 700 years ago.

A second little mystery presents itself even before you climb to the church: the presence of a long wooden footbridge that seems to span nothing but grass and

nettles. The solution can be found in the sky above. Come after a prolonged period of wet weather and you'll be glad you are able to cross dry-shod the winterbourne that rises here.

St Hubert's was not only built in pre-Norman times, it was built by the father of the man who tried so hard to ensure that there were no Norman times in England to speak of. Earl Godwine of Wessex died in 1053 but during his lifetime he had a hunting chapel constructed here on his own land at Idsworth and fathered 11 children, one of whom became Harold II of 1066 fame. Although much of the building we see today dates from the later Middle Ages, the flint north and west walls are Saxon.

Once you have enjoyed the view of the gentle valley below, perhaps with a train rattling through it, the exterior of the church offers up two points of interest. The southwest corner of the south wall, which is constructed of rubble and sandstone quoins, has what looks like a sundial scratched into it. However, this may well be a mass dial, an early form of noticeboard. The priest in charge would insert a bent twig in the central hole and the outer end would indicate the time of the next mass.

The other feature is very much more modern. The west and south walls have been recently rendered with a mix of lime mortar and crushed flint. Contrary to popular belief, this reflects what such churches would have looked like when built. The 'exposed' look is merely the result of render detaching itself over the centuries. An enlightening (and, it has to be said, somewhat defensive) notice inside the church explains the reasoning behind the brave decision to re-render.

For the vast majority of its life, the church was known as St Peter's (or possibly St Peter and St Paul's) but the dedication was changed to St Hubert – the patron saint of hunters – in the 19th century, probably after the discovery in 1864 of an extraordinary wall painting. It is that painting that immediately draws the eye on entering the chancel, where the unknown artist's deep yellows and pinky-reds light up the north wall.

Painted around 1330, it comprises an upper and a lower scene split by a thick zigzagged band, which unwittingly leaves modern viewers with the impression that they are looking at a cutaway of two rooms, one above the other, albeit that the one on top has trees growing in it. The lower scene represents the New Testament story in which Salome, having been pressed by her mother to ask her stepfather Herod for the head of his prisoner John the Baptist, is presented with it on a platter. On the far left we see the unfortunate John's delivery into the prison that was his final home on earth.

The subject of the upper portion of the painting is less clearly divined. While evidently a hunting scene, it may show St Hubert curing or possibly converting a lycanthrope – that is, a person who believes themself to be a wolf (we've all had days like that). Alternatively, we might be witnessing the arrest of John the Baptist at the far right, while the remainder of the painting deals with the trope of the 'hairy anchorite' or penitent who went about on all fours to atone for his sins.

Whichever interpretation is correct, the two scenes can also be neatly tied together by Oscar Wilde's aphorism

about hunters – 'the unspeakable in pursuit of the inedible' – a description that could just as easily be applied to Salome.

The chancel ceiling is adorned with 13 medallions in a diamond lattice. Every medallion bears a different motif, including the Good Shepherd, a sailing ship, and St Hubert and a stag (the saint was converted on seeing a vision of Christ in the antlers of such a beast).

If this were not enough, in the splayed east window there's another 1330 fresco to enjoy, depicting St Peter and St Paul: the former with his customary keys to heaven, the latter carrying a staff and a book.

To celebrate the new millennium, the church commissioned a 14th-century style fresco. It dominates the nave and shows 'Christ in Majesty' flanked by the sheet St Peter saw in his vision; a modern hunt (whose activities were to be outlawed four years later); various other wild animals, including a perky little badger; and, if you look carefully, one of the trains that speeds along the valley beneath the church.

On a wall below, a 1795 plan of the church shows the names of those renting each box (or 'seat room'). Some of the boxes have now been replaced by narrow and rather uncomfortable-looking pews. However, wherever you sit there's no possibility of not hearing the sermon. The Jacobean pulpit, unusually placed along one side of the nave, has a tester above it to aid amplification. This renders unnecessary the encouragement to the preacher posted on the wall beside it: 'Cry aloud, spare not, lift up thy voice like a trumpet...' (Isaiah 58:1). 🕷

ST MARY'S
NORTH MARDEN

Come for the Caen stone and be won over by the rather extraordinary tower.

SPIRITUAL ORIENTATION
Church of England

PHYSICAL ORIENTATION
North Marden, West Sussex
PO18 9JD
Grid reference: SU 807 161
OS Landranger map 197

PUBLIC TRANSPORT
Sadly, there are no bus services to North Marden. The hamlet is 8 miles from

Chichester railway station (southernrailway.com; 03451 272920). The church is to the west of the main road that runs through North Marden and is clearly signposted.

OPENING ARRANGEMENTS
Always open.

SERVICES
8pm 1st Thursday (Night Prayer).

here's probably never been a village at North Marden. A farm or two and a small cluster of cottages appears to have been the summit of its ambitions since its formation in Saxon times. It can therefore count itself lucky that for the majority of its existence it has been the proud possessor of a fine church with an apse. These semicircular constructions, which were usually built at the east end to accommodate the altar, never entered the mainstream of British church architecture, which is puzzling because they're often very attractive.

At St Mary's, the visual effect is exaggerated by the fact that the chancel

and nave are the same width. The wall is thus allowed to curl around in an organic fashion, mirroring the hills of the South Downs that are its home. It's not bad for a church that was built merely as a chapel of ease to save the sparse population the mile walk to East Marden.

Constructed in the 12th century of flint rubble with ashlar (cut stone) dressings, St Mary's is reckoned to have been established by one Geoffrey, son of Azo. Not one to stint on a project, Geoffrey had stone shipped all the way from Caen to Chichester, which was then lugged up into the hills by packhorse. With it he created a doorway into the church with a

Romanesque arch. Pevsner dates this to 1130–1140 from its elaborate saw-tooth and chevron patterns. The three windows in the apse are also fashioned from Caen stone and look convincingly late Norman, but are actually 19th-century counterfeits. These tend to be frowned upon by experts in ecclesiastical architecture as something akin to forgeries but, given the havoc inflicted upon churches by the Victorians across the country, St Mary's can consider itself to have got off very lightly.

Just inside the door, you'll find a font with a sandstone bowl that could well be original, though the octagonal stem on which it stands is probably 14th century. Meanwhile, the west wall features two wooden panels, each with twin Gothic arches. The first displays a Credo and Commandments one to four, while the second bears the latter six Commandments and the Lord's Prayer – and thus all the most needful theological bases are covered.

There is an unusual configuration of windows between the panels. A large arched window is chiefly composed of ochre and off-white glass that suffuses the church with a yellowy light when the sun shines through it. Above this is a very much smaller lancet which is the only original window in the church. It is fitted out with panes of clear, lilac and light blue glass, the effect of which is all but blotted

out by an unfortunately placed beam installed to keep the much more modern bell tower in place. A single bell rope hangs down tied in a small loop at the bottom, as if ready to hang some miscreant rabbit.

To the north, opposite the entrance, an arched doorway gives on to a vestry (like the porch, an unfortunate 19th-century addition). Beside it is a small and very humble brass plaque bearing the words:

> *Benjamin James Crees*
> *10-7-1915 – 25-9-1943*
> *118th Field Regiment Royal Artillery*
> *AOMI P.O.W. Camp, Japan*

The bald details mask a no-doubt harrowing story. Benjamin Crees was one of tens of thousands of Allied servicemen who died in prisoner of war camps on Japanese soil during World War II, often used as slave labour and kept alive on minimal rations.

The two windows on either side of the nave show Jesus in such popular stained-glass guises that they have long since become hackneyed. In the northerly one he stands at the door and knocks. In the other (conspicuously attired in the same clothes) he crooks a lamb in his arm above the legend 'I am the Good Shepherd'. If you look carefully at this south-facing window, you'll spot the church's own

chancel. The latter plays host to those three fake Norman windows. They are filled with brightly coloured glass in a pattern vaguely reminiscent of a child's toy, giving off an air of cheerfulness echoed by the colourful modern kneelers sitting on the pews. Four candles and a small simple cross stand on the plain altar.

To the right of the altar is a niche with a pointed trefoil head. This is also of Caen stone, though a century or two later than the doorway, and it would doubtless have accommodated a piscina or a statue. Since neither is present, to give it some purpose someone has placed in it a painting of the Virgin Mary holding an infant Jesus equipped with an unfeasibly small head. A slip of paper on the back of the painting reveals it to be a copy of one in the Palazzo Rocca in Venice. It also has the imprimatur of The Ruskin House of Art Appreciation, so it's probably best to pretend you like it even if it's not quite to your taste.

After looking at the church, if the weather is fine, do spend some time outside sitting on the bench that runs almost the whole width of its western end and bears the inscription: 'I am not leaving you – I am with you always – My heart is with you'. It enjoys a bucolic view across a valley to Fernbeds Down and Apple Down, and is just the place to spend a few moments of quiet contemplation.

stubby tower peeking above the trees in the background.

The small stone flags of the nave floor give way to tiles as you approach the altar, compensating a little for the fact that there is no arch to separate the nave from the

CHURCH OF THE GOOD SHEPHERD
LULLINGTON

The charming little churchyard affords a sumptuous view over the South Downs.

SPIRITUAL ORIENTATION
Church of England

PHYSICAL ORIENTATION
Chapel Hill, Lullington,
East Sussex BN26 5QX
Grid reference: TQ 528 030
OS Landranger map 199

PUBLIC TRANSPORT
From Polegate railway station (southernrailway.com; 03451 272920) take the no. 125 bus (compass-travel.co.uk; 01903 690025)

to Alfriston. From here, there is a delightful walk down River Lane, across the White Bridge and Lullington Road and uphill along the footpath opposite (by Great Meadow Barn) all the way to the church. If you wish to cycle, there is an alternative route from Polegate sans champs via the Wilmington to Litlington road. The way to the church is via an unmarked footpath running beside the garden fence of a house. NB There is no

parking available here or on the narrow road.

OPENING ARRANGEMENTS
Daily from 9am to 5pm or dusk.

SERVICES
3pm 3rd Sunday (Evensong) April to September (except June)
6.30am Easter Sunday
4.30pm (Lantern Service) 1st Sunday of Advent
For further details ring the St Andrew's parish office in Alfriston (01323 871093).

alf a mile east of Alfriston, high up in the South Downs above the Cuckmere Valley – one of the most attractive landscapes in England – sits a tiny scrap of a church. It's little more than a flint, chalk and mortar box topped with a steep roof and an endearing weatherboarded belfry, a building so small it looks like a model of a church rather than a real one.

The approach to it from the ancient village of Alfriston makes a visit even more memorable. Leaving behind the mighty St Andrew's – known as the Cathedral

of the Downs – the pilgrim crosses a footbridge over the Cuckmere River and takes a footpath that climbs through arable farmland to a stand of trees that includes one particularly fine ash. Such is the diminutive nature of the church that it cannot be seen until you are almost on top of it.

Though not the tiniest church in the country, as is often erroneously claimed, at about 16ft square it's still pretty small. However, it is cheating slightly because, as with the Old Church of St Mary the Virgin (p52), what is left to us today is merely the

chancel, the rest of the church having disappeared a long time since. Begun around 1180 and enlarged in about 1350, the church seems to have suffered a catastrophic fire, possibly during the period of Cromwell's Commonwealth. In 1893 the chancel was partially rebuilt – it having fared better than the nave in the fire – and a fresh wall closing off the front created the basis of the new church. There's enough room inside for 20 people, but when the popular Harvest Festival service is celebrated the congregation spills out into the small churchyard.

A good portion of the graveyard would once have been taken up by the nave and what might have been a porch, but there's very little left of either now. The walls either side of the chancel end rather abruptly, although the more southerly one at least continues for long enough to show us there was once a window in it. Other remnants are a couple of slivers of footings, a small fragment of wall about the length of a grave, and a slightly more substantial block that marks the old western end of the church. A further item of interest is a low brick-built structure

topped with two stone slabs. A rosemary bush – a plant traditionally grown 'for remembrance' – guards the door.

The church itself has five windows, four of which date from the 14th century, while the last, in the north side, is from the 13th. Inside, the stone that frames the windows and a small niche is cut from South Downs chalk. There is no electric light or heating and little room for anything but an unfussy altar and rail, a lectern and a harmonium, none of which are of any particular antiquity. Two photos show Lullington's parishioners grouped outside the church in 1993 and at its restoration in 1893, the latter image a flurry of large beards, top hats and black crêpe de Chine. An informative plan of the church created in the aftermath of an archeological study in 1970 shows the century to which each section belongs.

The dedication to the 'Good Shepherd' is an unusual one for an ancient church. It came about because there is some uncertainty as to the original dedication, if indeed there was one. Just one snippet of evidence suggests a saint may have been linked to the church. It's contained in a will from 1521 made by one Jegelian Hunt. He bequeathed a number of possessions to the church, including 'a taper sett before Saint Sithe in the same church'.

St Sithe is more commonly known as St Zita, a 13th-century serving girl from a village near Lucca in Italy. Her meekness and piety irked those around her to such an extent that they took against her. She eventually won her persecutors over and so was placed in charge of the household she served. Zita used her new-found influence to defend her fellow servants. All in all, she sounds like a very worthy human being but, as saintly lives go, it's not a thrilling read. At no point does she survive a shipwreck, or preach the gospel to bears, which perhaps accounts for her relative obscurity. Even assuming there was a statuette or image of this saint before which a taper (a small candle) could be set, that still wouldn't be sufficient to prove that the church wasn't dedicated to some other saint, or none.

In 1998, it was decided by the parish that Lullington Church, as it was then known, should be given a belated dedication. After exhaustive consultation a decision was made and, on 10 September 2000, the Bishop of Lewes conducted a service devoting the church to the Good Shepherd. It's a fitting moniker for this haven of peace and security among the flocks of sheep that graze the Downs.

ST THOMAS BECKET

FAIRFIELD

The first sight of this church is likely to make you catch your breath.

SPIRITUAL ORIENTATION
Church of England

PHYSICAL ORIENTATION
Fairfield, Romney Marsh, Kent TN29 9RZ
Grid reference: TQ 966 264
OS Landranger map 189

PUBLIC TRANSPORT
From Appledore railway station (southernrailway. com; 03451 272920) it's a 3.5-mile walk or cycle ride to the church, south along the B2080, then right down Snargate Lane. At the end, turn right to the house called Beckets to retrieve the church key (see below). On the way there you'll pass a short footpath to the church.

OPENING ARRANGEMENTS
The church is kept locked. The key hangs on the front wall of a house called Beckets which is 200yd west along the road from where the footpath meets the road to the west of the church. There is no need to ask to borrow the key but do remember to return it.

SERVICES
10am 1st Sunday of the month, except December. Further information from Rev Shuna Body (01797 343977).

et adrift among a maze of watercourses in a flat and barely populated corner of Romney Marsh, the church of St Thomas Becket is blessed with an atmospheric beauty enhanced by its desolate surroundings.

The steeply pitched red-tiled roof of the nave topped by a bell-cote that resembles a castle turret marks the building out from the common stock. If it looks familiar it may be because you have indeed seen it before. It featured in the BBC retelling of the Ford Madox Ford novel *Parade's End*, and both the recent television and cinema adaptations of Dickens' *Great Expectations*.

By rights it shouldn't be here at all. Fairfield – a locality wonderfully written off by the 18th-century historian Edward Hasted as 'a most unpleasant and dreary place... far from what its name seems to imply' – has always had an atomised population and so its church was built with the idea that it might not be needed for very long. Thus a small lath and plaster structure was first thrown up on this spot at a date that is, perhaps understandably, unrecorded, though it would have been some time around 1200. However, there always seems to have been just enough people in the surrounding area to sustain a place of worship and the church today is the result of many building efforts over the centuries, though overall what we see is the church as it was in the 18th century.

Unfortunately, perhaps because they still believed the structure was merely temporary, the various 18th-century builders did a rather slipshod job when they encased the timber frames in brick.

The inherent dampness of the marsh did the church no favours either, and in 1912 it was found to be on the verge of falling down. In order to save it, the vast majority of the building was completely disassembled and reconstructed. The success of this radical undertaking is that it is now nigh on impossible to tell what of

the external work is ancient and what is merely a century or so old, with the exception of the porch, whose materials were beyond saving, and the bell-turret which now sports cedar shingles rather than weatherboarding, and had to be slightly redesigned.

The building, which is the smallest complete church in the county, has also been at the mercy of the waters that surround it. Although it stands on an artificial mound, until a causeway was created in 1913 it was habitually encircled by water in winter and spring as if it were a moated castle. As a result, worshippers often had to resort to a boat in order to attend services. Even after matters were improved by the causeway (which also provides one of the access routes to the church), a flood in November 1960 turned the surrounding fields into what appears to be a limitless sea, as captured in a newspaper photograph that hangs on the wall. Hapless and helpless, the church looks like a capsized Noah's ark.

St Thomas Becket's is accessible from two directions by footpath via reassuringly sturdy modern bridges. Before going inside, have a look at the 18th-century mounting block installed for the convenience of those travelling to services by horse, an indicator of just how scattered the congregation was at that time.

The church is one of a handful in England dedicated to St Thomas à Becket, including another fine example at Capel, near Tonbridge. Becket was Archbishop of Canterbury for eight years from 1162 until famously murdered in his own cathedral by four knights keen to become the answer to Henry II's (possibly rhetorical) question, 'Have I no friend who will rid me of this upstart priest?' While the Becketian connection suggests that visitors might be in for a medieval experience, the interior actually plunges them into a largely Georgian world.

The plain rectangular windows give the place a homely feel, enhanced by the smartly painted box pews – bright white with a black trim – that fill both sides of the nave. High above them, tacked to the underside of the exposed roof, are text boards bearing improving Bible verses. Behind the altar are further boards, probably a little later than Georgian, that offer any congregants bored by a tediously prolix sermon the chance to brush up on the Lord's Prayer, the Ten Commandments and the Apostles' Creed.

The crowning moment is the Georgian three-decker pulpit, said to be the only one of its kind in Kent. As with a similar pulpit in Yorkshire (St Mary's, Lead, p168), the bottom section was reserved for the parish clerk while the priest would occupy the middle section for most of the service, rising to the top deck to preach his sermon.

The plain font with its heptagonal bowl is, however, medieval, dating from the 13th century. The reason for it having seven sides is obscure but may refer to the seven sacraments of the church.

Although you may not notice it, the chancel is set at a slight angle to the nave. This might have been to ensure that the church faced precisely eastwards, assuming the nave hadn't been positioned quite accurately enough. Alternatively, the 13th-century builders knew exactly what they were doing and chose to represent,

in architectural form, the image of Christ's head bowed to the left as he hung on the cross. This was a common enough practice so is the most plausible explanation for what might otherwise appear to be an oddity.

However, this is not a church to analyse and pick apart but rather one to enjoy, for there can be few more atmospheric buildings in such apparently remote and unworldly settings in all of England.

ST ANDREW'S
GREENSTED

A chance to see the oldest wooden church in the world in a humble corner of Essex.

SPIRITUAL ORIENTATION

Church of England

PHYSICAL ORIENTATION

Greensted-juxta-Ongar,
Essex CM5 9LD
Grid reference: TL 538 029
OS Landranger map 177

PUBLIC TRANSPORT

From Epping underground station (tfl.gov.uk; 0343 2221234) take a 21 bus (townlinkbuses.com; 01279 426266) to Chipping Ongar High Street (or treat yourself and take a steam train from Epping to Ongar – eorailway.co.uk; 01277 365200). Directly opposite the library is the Essex Way, a footpath that will take you westwards across fields directly to the church, just a mile away.

OPENING ARRANGEMENTS

Open daily. In summer from around 10am to 6pm; in winter from around 10am to 4pm.

SERVICES

9.30am Sunday (Matins, Holy Communion or a Family Service).

 f you ever needed proof that Britain has an embarrassment of riches when it comes to ancient buildings, you need look no further than this self-effacing corner of Essex. Here, without fanfare, and barely even signposted, stands the world's oldest wooden church. It also happens to be the oldest timber structure in Europe still standing. That didn't stop the Normans, Tudors and (inevitably) Victorians messing about with it but at least we can be thankful that none of them decided to burn it to the ground and start again.

The influence of each group on the church is more or less discrete, so walking from the entrance up the aisle is like engaging in a bit of gentle time travel. The Saxon nave gives way to a largely Tudor chancel beyond which is a Victorian sanctuary. It's only here that things start to get a little muddled by the presence of a restored 15th-century window and a Norman piscina.

The church is just about Saxon – the oldest among the 51 oak logs in situ date from six years before the advent of William the Conqueror. However, its roots are deeply embedded in that age: excavations carried out under the sanctuary in 1960 revealed evidence of two very small sanctuaries from the 6th or early 7th century. This takes the site back to around the time of St Cedd (see St Peter-on-the-Wall, p88, and St Fursey's, p106), who began his evangelistic mission among the Anglo-Saxons around 654. Preachers would hold forth from these simple structures – the walls built by dropping logs end-on into a trench – while those who cared to listen stood around and about. The nave was added in about

1060, at last providing shelter to those congregating, and was built using more sophisticated techniques. However, that sophistication did not run to windows – there were just a few simple eye-holes bored into the walls.

Though the Normans made some alterations, there is almost nothing left of their work here beyond a piscina and some footings. It was the Tudors who really left their mark. They completely rebuilt the chancel in brick; replaced the thatch with tiles; and added windows to admit natural light into the church for the first time.

The Victorian intervention was, inevitably, a less happy affair. Although the rector, Philip Ray, can be credited with recognising the importance of the somewhat ramshackle church he took charge of in 1837, the restoration he put into effect was, even at the time, viewed by some as overly intrusive. It included removing three Tudor windows and replacing them with six dormer windows; entirely reconstructing the porch and sanctuary; stripping the medieval plaster from the log walls; and installing stained-glass windows – changes that drastically altered the complexion of the church, albeit that the dormer windows give it an undeniably welcoming look.

There is some debate as to who was responsible for building the tower and spire. One of the church bells is inscribed 'William Land made me 1618' and it's possible that the tower went up at the same time. However, there are churches in the area with earlier towers and it may be that St Andrew's had one itself before that particular bell was installed. For all the alterations made to the church over the ages, it is the bright white tower with its black-tiled spire that is the only element that seems out of place. It's elegant enough, and the use of wood as the building material for the tower is highly appropriate, but it does rather look like someone has tried to jam a windmill onto the end of the church and has merely forgotten to add the sails.

Before going in, take a look at the grave to the right of the entrance. Here lies a 12th-century crusader and a celebrated one at that. We know this from his location by the south wall and the effort and expense taken in hauling stone here for his coffin.

For a church dedicated to St Andrew, there's an awful lot of St Edmund to be found inside. Just to the left of the entrance a 15th-century quatrefoil window above the door to the tower has what may be a depiction of the saint. His death features in a medieval-style painting on the north wall. Just above that is the 'St Edmund beam', carved by Victorian hands with the saint's emblems. To top it off, he stars in his own window. By contrast, St Andrew is commemorated just

the once – and even then his window faces St Edmund across the chancel.

The reason for all this Edmundophilia is that the remains of the martyred saint and former king of the East Angles stopped here in 1013 on the way to what is now Bury St Edmunds. He's by no means the only martyr with connections to the church though. When protests against the transportation of the Tolpuddle Martyrs to Australia resulted in their return to England in 1837, some became tenant farmers in Greensted. Two years later the church was the venue for the wedding of one of the men, James Brine, who married Elizabeth Standfield, daughter of another.

This church at Greensted, which once stood in the midst of an enormous forest ('stede' denoting a clearing), now lies on the Essex Way. There's a pouch of plastic bags in the porch for walkers to put over their muddy boots so they can explore the church without dirtying it. They can also quench their thirst with cartons of juice for sale inside, and lighten their wallets acquiring the excellent full-colour guidebook, homemade jams, jellies and mustards, and that most mystifyingly popular among souvenirs, the humble tea towel. St Cedd, being a thoroughly practical kind of saint, would certainly have approved.

ST MARY'S
MUNDON

While the 16th-century porch is excellent, the tower and its remarkable three-sided skirt is an extraordinary thing to behold.

SPIRITUAL ORIENTATION
Church of England (Friends of Friendless Churches)

PHYSICAL ORIENTATION
Vicarage Lane, Mundon, Essex CM9 6PA
Grid reference: TL 879 026
OS Landranger map 168

PUBLIC TRANSPORT
It's somewhat difficult to get to Mundon by public transport. The nearest railway station (5 miles) is North Fambridge, though from South Woodham Ferrers railway station (both abelliogreateranglia.co.uk; 0345 6007245) there is the FC07 bus (fordscoaches.co.uk; 01621 740326), but this only runs once a day and only on school days. In Mundon, leave the main road via a road named West Chase. This quickly gives way to a footpath (part of St Peter's Way) across a field. At the far end, continue along the road. Where it bends left to lead into a house, take a track off to the right to the church.

OPENING ARRANGEMENTS
Always open.

SERVICES
Occasional services are held in the church. For details, contact Friends of Friendless Churches (020 7236 3934).

In 1970, when St Mary's was declared redundant, it was being pulled apart by the marshy shifting ground beneath it. Large cracks had appeared in the walls and the collapse of the chancel was only a matter of time, and not a great deal of time either.

The church was constructed in the 14th century but there may have been a place of worship on this spot from Saxon times. The building is inside a moated area that also encompasses the neighbouring Mundon Hall. This slim channel of water would have offered at least a little protection from any raiding Norsemen who squelched across the marshes of the Dengie Peninsula to do some light pillaging. When the current church was built it would also have been surrounded by a village. The plague of 1665 caused its disappearance, not because it wiped out the entire population but because the villagers blamed the marsh for spreading the plague and so decamped to escape its supposedly pestilential vapours. If you approach St Mary's from the west you will pass through the new Mundon village they created.

The fact that the church is tucked away behind trees means that your first sight of it comes at very close quarters. That initial view is rather spectacular because it involves a sudden confrontation with the church's most arresting feature: its early 16th-century weatherboarded timber-framed belfry tower. No prosaic straight-walled tower this – on three sides it sports an enormous skirt. It is roofed with dashing vermillion tiles and its walls are a custard yellow.

The timber porch, just around the corner, was built at about the same time and is reckoned to be one of the finest in Essex. Look for the pendants hanging from the gable and the intricate wooden carvings. Do not be dismayed that the door here is locked because access to the church is through an entrance in the west side of the tower.

After all the finery outside, the interior of the church has a seductively louche feel to it, as if it has seen something of the

world and now bears the beautiful scars. There are fragments of medieval wall paintings in which a devil and a king appear; beneath the tower the buttresses that were demurely covered by the voluminous skirt are at last revealed; and the rubble and plaster nave, which is probably 14th century, hosts a mysterious blocked archway on its south side that led to a chapel, long since demolished. This all makes the plain octagonal font seem out of place, for it is a vision of minimalistic purity. It may be from around 1200 and thus an interloper from another church.

The 18th century saw the last major alterations to St Mary's. The brick chancel is from this period, as are the pulpit, the complete and well-preserved set of box pews and the oval murals bearing biblical texts. The choir stalls, though they match the box pews perfectly and seem of a piece, are actually from the following century. Behind them it all gets a little quirky. Look up on the east wall of the chancel and you'll see that it's covered with a naïve mural of curtains drawn back as if the window were a stage. It's a rare piece of rustic *trompe l'oeil* executed by some peripatetic Georgian muralist. One can easily imagine the novelist Leo Tolstoy enjoying the touch of the theatrical the painting gives the church when he visited during a trip to Essex in 1861.

Ninety-nine years later, the church received a visit from another writer, the journalist Bea Howe, and a copy of the *Country Life* article she composed afterwards can be found in the tower. She writes poignantly of peering through a broken window onto a scene of desolation: abandoned birds' nests, cobwebs and mildewed prayer books. The church, she reports, had been damaged by one of Hitler's V rockets in 1944. Given the building's isolated location far from any possible target, this was a piece of extraordinary bad luck. The fabric of the church was repaired in 1949 but this barely arrested its decline, as Howe's pen portrait demonstrates, and it was abandoned completely in 1970. Five years later the Friends of Friendless Churches took St Mary's on, arriving just in time to save it before the shifting marshes did their worst.

Before you tramp back to the modern world, take a few minutes to gaze upon a stand of ancient oaks to the east of the church. This is called the Old Grove and is traditionally believed to have been planted at about the same time the moat was dug, though this would make the trees the most venerable oaks in Britain by several hundred years, so that's unlikely. However, their wizened outlines give the impression that they're not quite of our time and not quite of our world, making them the ideal companions for the church with which they have grown old. 🔲

ST PETER-ON-THE-WALL
BRADWELL-ON-SEA

The simple comeliness of what is the oldest surviving cathedral in Britain is matched by the understated beauty of its location.

SPIRITUAL ORIENTATION
Church of England

PHYSICAL ORIENTATION
Bradwell-on-Sea,
Essex CM0 7PN
Grid reference: TM 031 081
OS Landranger map 168

PUBLIC TRANSPORT
At 9 miles, Southminster is the closest railway station to St Peter's but has no direct bus link to Bradwell-on-Sea. However, from the more distant Marks Tey station (abelliogreateranglia.co.uk; 0345 6007245) you can take the no. 70 bus (firstgroup. com; 0345 6020121). From St Thomas's church in Bradwell village it's 2 miles to St Peter's. Take the East End Road to its east end, where a footpath towards the sea leads directly to the church. Alternatively, choose a fine day and take the train to Burnham-on-Crouch from where you can walk along a coastal footpath all the way to the church (13 miles).

OPENING ARRANGEMENTS
Always open.

SERVICES
Every Sunday in July and August, and a candlelit carol service in December
An annual pilgrimage/festival also takes place on the 1st Saturday in July
See bradwellchapel.org for details, or contact Chaplain Rev Brigid Main (01621 776438).

The nearby Othona Community holds brief services in the chapel on most days. See othona-bradwell.org.uk for details.

he phrase 'once seen never forgotten' is one that is woefully over-used, but in the case of St Peter-on-the-Wall there might be some justification in giving it an airing. A bold landmark on a flat landscape, the chapel looks out over a large expanse of marshes that give way to a horizon untrammelled but for the distant hint of a wind farm far out into the North Sea.

It is less a church and more a full stop declaring to the countless pilgrims who have travelled here over the span of 14 centuries that this is their journey's end, their heart's desire. The fact that it resembles a rather tall barn only makes it all the more memorable and adds a certain pathos too, given what fate had in store for it.

The history of St Peter's begins in 653, over two centuries after the last Roman soldiers had pulled out of Britannia. It was in that year that a young priest called Cedd (see St Andrew's, Greensted, p78, and St

Fursey's, p106) sailed from Holy Island to Essex. Founding a Christian community of men and women by the ruins of a Roman fort called Othona, he raised up the Cathedral of St Peter on the foundations of the old gatehouse, which explains the suffix the church bears today.

Having initially built a wooden structure, he replaced it the following year with one of stone and brick plundered from the fort. Today it is the nation's oldest surviving cathedral. Cedd, who became Bishop to the East Saxons, died of the plague 10 years later at Lastingham, a community he founded in Northumbria. Thirty monks from Othona who visited Cedd on his deathbed are said to have contracted the disease from him. Just one young lad survived to return home to Essex. Regardless of this rather unfortunate end to his life, Cedd went on to be canonised. Despite his achievements, the history books have always favoured his brother, Chad, who became a bishop, a saint and ultimately an entire country.

Two years after William's successful, if rather fortunate, victory near Hastings, St Peter's was given to the St Valéry Benedictine Monastery in the Somme. Three centuries later it was bought by another William, this one not of Normandy but of Wykeham in Hampshire. He was the founder of New College, Oxford and at various times was Bishop of Winchester and Lord Chancellor. A tower (since disappeared) was built at some point prior to 1442, but by then the building had been badly damaged in a fire and was unserviceable. We also know that it once sported an apse with a porticus on either side (the foundations can still be traced in the grass) and a porch to the west, but these have all long since melted away. The church was repaired but, in 1750, we find that the once important cathedral had for some considerable time been used as a barn. A glance at the north and south walls is enough to make out the obvious outline of the massive doorways cut for this purpose. It was only as recently

as 1920 that the cattle were shooed from its precincts and the farm building became a place of worship again.

Although it may not be obvious, Cedd took his inspiration for the design of his church from those built in Egypt and Syria. Given its exposed location, the structure has withstood the buffeting of countless sea gales remarkably well, and is a testament to the Saxon builders as well as the Romano-Britons who made the bricks and cut the stone. The red-tiled roof has fared rather worse: major repairs had to be carried out in 1947 and again in 2015.

Inside, the short but high-ceilinged nave is dominated by a Byzantine-style icon high up on the east wall that depicts Christ on the cross with St Cedd kneeling below. It was installed around 1949 and was created by the artist Francis William Stephens. Below it stands an impressive stone altar. It has three stones set into its front, each one representing a community with links to St Cedd. The left-hand stone comes from Holy Island, the middle stone is from Iona (where all Celtic mission in Britain has its roots), while the right-hand stone hails from Lastingham. Little else intrudes on this remarkable space – just a handful of benches on the grey stone flags and some minor fixtures (all modern) on the walls. There is an overwhelming sense that you are not only somewhere ancient but also somewhere holy, despite its agricultural past. To experience the church at its very best, though, come for the annual carol service when it is lit by candlelight and you see it just as those women and men from Cedd's plucky little community saw it over 1,350 years ago. 🗒

17 ST PETER'S
CAMBRIDGE

Seek out the stone font to see four mermen clutching their tails.

SPIRITUAL ORIENTATION
Church of England (Churches Conservation Trust)

PHYSICAL ORIENTATION
Castle Hill, Cambridge, Cambridgeshire CB3 0AJ
Grid reference: TL 444 592
OS Landranger map 154

PUBLIC TRANSPORT
From Cambridge railway station it's a 1.75-mile walk through the centre of Cambridge to St Peter's. Alternatively, you can take the Citi 8 bus (stagecoachbus.com; 01223 433250) to the first Histon Road bus stop, which is very close to the church.

OPENING ARRANGEMENTS
9am–noon Monday 11am–5pm Tuesday to Sunday. At other times a key is available from Kettle's Yard gallery next door.

SERVICES
Occasional. See churchatcastle.org for details.

very city needs its oases of calm. St Peter's, garlanded with wild flowers and standing on a tiny grassy knoll amid mature limes and horse chestnuts, provides a little haven for the good people of northwest Cambridge.

It's appropriate that it brings something of the bucolic to the university town because when it was built it had one foot in the countryside. There's no certainty as to the exact year in which it came into being but it would have been around the same time or soon after the establishment in 1068 of William the Conqueror's nearby castle, the mound of which can still be visited. Two other churches – St Giles' and All Saints-by-the-Castle – were erected at around the same time.

The interior is no more than a handful of strides in each direction, making it the smallest medieval church in Cambridge by some margin. The fact that it still exists at all is something of a miracle and the story of how such a minute building came to have such a disproportionately tall spire – one that is very much part of the Cambridge skyline – is an interesting one.

From its construction, St Peter's oversaw a poor parish, a state of affairs that hasn't changed materially over the centuries. However, by 1350 it had defied its humble origins and the ravages of the Black Death the year before to grow to the largest size it would ever attain. The church boasted a nave, a chancel, a south porch, a south aisle and a tower topped with a spire.

The church found itself at the centre of a scandal in 1461. One Henry Akenborough sought sanctuary in the churchyard (as was the right of any citizen) but was summarily hauled off by the mayor of Cambridge, two bailiffs and seven locals and thrown into the town tollbooth. Akenborough was only reluctantly escorted back to the churchyard when the Bishop of Ely threatened to excommunicate those responsible for his incarceration.

St Peter's downfall began with the Reformation. The sudden lack of a need for chapels made the church's south aisle expendable and it was duly knocked down.

During the Civil War, St Peter's was caught up in the struggles between the Anglicans and the Puritans. As part of Archbishop Laud's campaign to accentuate Anglican ritual throughout the land, Bishop Matthew Wren had commanded some minor changes to the arrangement of the pulpit and communion table at the church. However, when the Parliamentarian forces took over in Cambridge, St Peter's had a visit from the Puritan orthodoxy police, in the shape of William Dowsing and his somewhat less than merry men. Dowsing recorded the incident in his journal:

At St Peter's parish December 30 [1643] we brake downe ten popish pictures; we took three popish

inscriptions for prayers to be made for their soules, and burnt the rayles, diged up the steps, and they are to be levelled on Wednesday.

This led to a series of very close shaves for St Peter's. In 1650, there was a plan to demolish the church and for its parishioners to attend nearby St Giles', but it came to nothing. Even so, visiting the church in 1772, Rev William Cole reported that:

This church is now a ruin, with no roof or peice [sic] of glass about it; and has been suffered to lye thus these 15 or 16 years.

An appeal for funds to restore the church went out but by 1780 an architect called James Essex noted that:

... they were going to pull down the walls of this church to mend the roads to the Castle Hill by the Backway.

A year later, the church received a reprieve of sorts. It was kept open and repaired but, at the same time, trimmed to roughly a third of its previous dimensions, the size it has remained ever since.

Visit the church today and among the first things you'll notice are the cross-shaped iron tie-bars doing their best to keep both the nave and the tower from

collapse. This is not altogether surprising since the tower is constructed from flint rubble, stones and occasional tiles salvaged from the Roman town of Durolipons in whose southwest corner the church stands. The 14th-century spire that sits on it is, by contrast, much more prudently built from finished limestone. The western side of the nave is original (the eastern side dates from the 1781 reworking) and is a mixture of flint, Northamptonshire limestone and Roman tiles.

Peer upwards to the top of the spire and you'll make out a weathervane. It bears the initials A P, standing for Andrew Perne, Master of Peterhouse (1554–89) and Dean of Ely (1557–89). He was known as the 'weathercock dean' for his astounding ability to curry favour with whichever political or religious cabal held sway at any time. The wits of the day claimed his initials stood for 'A Protestant, A Puritan or A Papist'.

The south doorway, though plain, is an absolute delight. Dating from the early 13th century it comprises an arch of two separate roll mouldings with a pair of simple round colonettes on both sides, their capitals adorned with leaves. Pass through it and you enter a temple to minimalism: a floor of flagstones, whitewashed walls and a boarded ceiling from which hangs a modern chandelier supporting 18 candles. The north wall contains a blocked doorway that is probably 12th century.

The eye is drawn ineluctably to the 12th-century font, which somehow passed muster with the Puritan hit squad despite the fact that its square bowl is adorned with four mermen, each of whom has grabbed one part of his forked tail. While the link between mermen and the immersion in water that occurs at christenings is an obvious one, this is a design you'll rarely see in Britain, although it's popular in French Romanesque churches. Almost the only other decoration within the church is provided by the east window's stained glass with its floral patterns and roundels. This is the work of late-Victorian artist Frederick Richard Leach.

But we cannot leave St Peter's without mentioning Jim Ede, who founded Kettle's Yard gallery next door and who was responsible for a great many repairs to the church in the 20th century and for its interior design. It's a fitting tribute that artists are often commissioned to install work within the church. Beside the altar you'll see a memorial stone to Ede that includes the final two lines of an Edmund Spenser sonnet:

So let us love, dear love, like as we ought,
Love is the lesson that the Lord us taught.

18 ST ANDREW'S
FRENZE

Look out for the medieval carvings, including two rather cheery little monkeys.

SPIRITUAL ORIENTATION

Church of England (Churches Conservation Trust)

PHYSICAL ORIENTATION

Frenze Hall Lane, Frenze, Diss, Norfolk IP21 4EZ
Grid reference: TM 135 804
OS Landranger map 144

PUBLIC TRANSPORT

The church is just a mile from Diss railway station (abelliogreateranglia.co.uk; 0345 6007245). Leave the car park by a small unofficial-looking path opposite the station buildings, head along Nelson Road and turn left along Sandy Lane at the roundabout. Turn right off the road along the Angles Way byway until you reach a footbridge that crosses a stream just beyond a ford. The church is directly opposite.

OPENING ARRANGEMENTS

Open daily.

SERVICES

Two a year: an Evening Prayer (and picnic) in May or June, and a Carols by Candlelight one evening in Advent
For further details contact the local benefice office (01379 741994).

he best way to approach St Andrew's is from the north. A byway will take you to a point where you can cross a footbridge over a stream – a little tributary of the Waveney – or, if you fancy a paddle, you can wade over a nearby ford. Whichever way you choose, you'll find the view you get of this humble rubble-and-flint vernacular church, of which only the nave and a porch survive, truly heart-warming. Sitting in a small field of buttercups and speedwell, from a distance it might almost be mistaken for a farm building were it not for the bell turret. Indeed, the 18th-century Norfolk historian Francis Blomefield thought that many a would-be church looter had probably been deceived by its barn-like mien.

Built in the 13th century, possibly at the behest of a lord of the manor called John de Lowdham, St Andrew's, along with the neighbouring farm, has outlived the great hall to which it was attached. There are two reasons why the church is so small. Firstly, the population of Frenze appears to have peaked at 60 (in just six houses!) in 1736 and has habitually been a fraction of that; and secondly, in 1827, when the church's eastward-facing chancel was in need of repair, it was deemed surplus to requirements and demolished. The walls that remain are considerably wider at the bottom than at the top, a building style called 'battered'. They are held up by numerous buttresses and tie-beams that have been added piecemeal over the centuries.

There are just four main windows. The two at the north and south are from the early 14th century and are in the Decorated style, while there is a smaller arched window at the east end of the north wall. It's interesting to note that glaziers responsible for repairing the windows have left their names on some of the panes. In the main north window, one of the workmen – clearly also an amateur meteorologist – found it necessary to add: 'Saturday afternoon windy'.

The church is entered via a sturdy brick porch built in Tudor times. According to Pevsner, Margaret James bequeathed a cow to the church in 1521 to pay for its repair. Look down by the door to see two damaged medieval coffin lids.

Given its unassuming exterior, you might be forgiven for expecting something similar within. However, that is the trick St Andrew's likes to play on visitors, for inside there is a treasure trove of beautiful brasses, centuries-old pews with delightful carvings including two little monkeys, a medieval sanctuary ring, and an imposing pulpit with a sounding board or tester.

A stall, squire's pew and pulpit are all Jacobean and made of oak that the years have turned beige and silver. A banner draped from the pulpit implores visitors to 'Climb Up and Read Aloud' to test the

efficacy of the hexagonal sounding board, a simple but effective piece of 17th-century acoustic technology.

When you have finished declaiming, on top of the altar you'll find a stone mensa from the Middle Ages that has five consecration crosses etched into it, representing the wounds of the crucified Christ in his hands, feet and side. After the Reformation the mensa fell into disfavour and for several hundred years saw service

as a doorstep. On its discovery during repairs made to the church in 1900 it was restored to its original position.

At the other end of the church is the font, which is probably 14th century, the same age as the north and south windows. Its design echoes the tracery found on them. Continuing on a watery theme, beneath each of those windows you'll find a piscina, the one beneath the north window coming with a fancy trefoil design. These would have had various uses connected with the giving of mass, most notably in providing a place for the ritual washing of vessels or of the priest's hands.

One of John de Lowdham's descendants was a woman called Joan who died in 1501 at the exceptional age of 97 having lived through all or part of the reigns of Henrys IV, V, VI and VII, Edwards IV and V, and Richard III (albeit not in that order). She married Ralph Blennerhasset, who came from the Cumberland village of the same name. Most of the wonderful brasses in the church commemorate members of the Blennerhasset family, who had connections with the church up until 1636. Of particular interest is that of Mary who first married Thomas Culpeper (not the one who was executed for his alleged relations with Catherine Howard) and then the statesman, philosopher and scientist Francis Bacon, though sadly she did not live to see the latter truly make his name. On the back of the various components of her brass is an image of an unknown scholar from the early 15th century.

In 1637, the Frenze estate changed hands. If you thought the world was badly served by having had one Richard Nixon in it, here you will find the remains of two more. They are Richard Nixon senior, who purchased the estate and died in the memorable year of 1666, and his son of the same name, who passed away just 12 years later.

However, it would be a shame to end your visit with such infelicitous associations running through your head, so take a moment or two to seek out the pair of wooden monkeys. You'll find them on the arms of a 17th-century stall, though they themselves were carved two centuries earlier. The cheeky little fellows provide a welcome balance to the stiffness of the brasses and chime well with the church's informal exterior. 🐒

ALL SAINTS
KESWICK

East Anglia's smallest Anglican church plays host to the nation's most comical font.

SPIRITUAL ORIENTATION
Church of England

PHYSICAL ORIENTATION
B1113, near Keswick, Norfolk NR4 6TP
Grid reference: TG 213 047
OS Landranger map 134

PUBLIC TRANSPORT
From Norwich railway station (abelliogreateranglia.co.uk; 0345 6007245) it's 3.75 miles southwest to the church, which is in a field just off the B1113 half a mile from Keswick village. Walk from the station to Castle Meadow and take the 37 bus (firstgroup.com; 0345 6020121) to Keswick and ask the driver to set you down at the stop on the B1113 nearest to the church. Keep your eyes peeled for a small sign advertising the church by a gap in the hedge. Alternatively, take the no. 2 bus (simonds.co.uk; 01379 647300) from the railway station to the Tesco superstore on the Ipswich Road and walk to the church.

OPENING ARRANGEMENTS
Contact Rev Paul Burr in nearby Swardeston to arrange a visit (01508 570550).

SERVICES
11am 2nd Sunday (Morning Prayer)
8am 4th Sunday (Holy Communion) except at Christmas, Easter and in August
9am Remembrance Sunday and Christmas Day.

oor old Keswick. Not only is this not the famous Keswick in the Lake District, it's not even the most well known Keswick in Norfolk – that one is by the coast near Bacton. This particular Keswick is about 3 miles south of Norwich and its one claim to fame – All Saints Church – is not even in the village but a full half-mile outside it.

The smallest working Anglican church in East Anglia sits daintily in a field, hidden behind a stand of trees a little way off the anonymous B1113. Built in the 9th or 10th century and dedicated to the Virgin Mary, it boasts one of the architectural specialities of the region: a round tower. It also comes with a history more chequered than most, as is immediately apparent to all who visit, for there is a fragmentary medieval wall standing adrift of the main church, which itself is largely Saxon and Victorian.

The estate on which the church stands came into the hands of Sir Henry Hobart, who set about demolishing the dilapidated structure in 1602. To add insult to injury, he used it as a quarry for stones to restore the round-towered church at Intwood, near his home. This left St Mary's a romantic ruin – only a wall of the nave, a section of the chancel and part of the tower remained. It mouldered away for nearly 300 years and may well have disappeared entirely had it not been for the arrival on the scene of John Henry Gurney. Having been thrown out of the staunchly pacifist Society of Friends (Quakers) for giving alms to soldiers, he joined the Anglican Church. Inheriting the ruin as part of his father's estate, he made a decision in 1893 to restore it for use as the family's mortuary chapel. He repaired the tower (whose belfry is 15th century rather than Saxon) and built a nave to keep it company, incorporating the surviving western wall. At a later date he opened up the graveyard to the local populace as an Anglican burial ground.

Visitors today pass through a gate guarded by two substantial though relatively young yews. Beyond, a few strides away from the church, looms the original east wall of the chancel. A bench now sits roughly where the altar would have been and on sunny days makes for a pleasant place to sit and reflect.

The church began holding services again in 1920 at the instigation of Gerard Hudson Gurney, when it had no apse, making it even smaller than it is today. Once you have got over the disorientation produced by the nave being slightly wider than it is long, there are two points of interest to look out for, and a maligned piece of art to consider.

A must-see is the font, which is – to use an adjective not often used of fonts – hilarious. Fitted out with two ineffectual-

looking handles and inexpertly engraved with a virtually blank crest flanked by a lion and what looks like a terrified pony, it has all the hallmarks of a cheap garden ornament. The object was donated by Gerard Gurney, and it is to be supposed that he discovered it somewhere on his estate and found it too hideous to live with, so packed it off to Keswick to give everyone a giggle.

The second foible has a more sombre mien. If you stoop down and look at the pews at the front of the church you'll notice that the legs are hinged. This was because the church was so small before the apse was added in 1964 that the only way a coffin could be turned around was by folding back the front pews.

The window above the apse is wont to divide opinion. Depicting Hope, it shows a figure holding an anchor (see St Leonard's, Chapel-le-Dale, p184) and was installed by the William Morris workshop in 1922. It was dismissed by Pevsner as 'very ordinary', though the same authority also got John Henry Gurney's name completely wrong (he refers to him as Herbert Green) and was five years out when dating the demolition of the church, so perhaps we might allow ourselves the luxury of ignoring the great man's views in this case.

Meanwhile, two golden and red angels mounted on the wall of the apse are of unknown origin but the rather more modest scarlet-winged angels up in the rafters are from the 15th century.

The church was dedicated to All Saints in 1964 and, for all that it is a curious admixture of Saxon and late Victorian with a little medieval thrown in, the overall effect is really rather delightful. 🦋

ST FURSEY'S
SUTTON

It's difficult to decide whether the highlight of a trip here is seeing inside this wonderfully crafted miniature version of a basilica or meeting its priest and builder.

SPIRITUAL ORIENTATION
Antiochian Orthodox

PHYSICAL ORIENTATION
St Fursey's House, 111 Neville Road, Sutton, Norfolk NR12 9RR
Grid reference: TG 380 241
OS Landranger map 133

PUBLIC TRANSPORT
Travel to either North Walsham railway station or Hoveton and Wroxham station (both abelliogreateranglia.co.uk; 0345 6007245). From the former, take the no. 6 bus (sanderscoaches.com; 01263 712800) to the stop opposite Moor Road, Sutton. From the latter, board a no. 10 bus (also Sanders) to the same stop from outside Roy's Department Store in Wroxham. Walk up Moor Road, left along the Old Yarmouth Road and left again into Neville Road. No. 111 is on the left in a row of houses reached by a footpath beside no. 117.

OPENING ARRANGEMENTS
Ring Father Stephen (01692 580552) to arrange a visit or turn up to a service.

SERVICES
Brief daily services are held at 9am, noon, 4pm and 9pm, with longer services on Saturday at 4pm (Vespers) and Sunday at 10am (Divine Liturgy).

The smallest working church in England and arguably the strangest, St Fursey's is a modern-day labour of love. While churches such as St Edwold's (p30) and St John's, Little Gidding (p120), appear to have been built in a back garden, in this case it is literally true, the garden in question belonging to its priest, Father Stephen Weston. Constructed mainly of plywood, it measures just 18ft by 13ft. Among churches in frequent use only St Trillo's (p251) is smaller, and there they hold only a couple of services a week whereas over the same period St Fursey's celebrates nigh on 30.

The story began in 1998 when Father Stephen, disillusioned with the Anglican Church in which he had served as a vicar for 20 years, left to join the Antiochian Orthodox Church. There being no English-speaking Orthodox church in the district – the closest being in Norwich – he immediately set about constructing one, putting an A-level in woodwork gained during his 40s to good use. Basing the design on an almost equally small 4th-century church at Silchester in

Hampshire, with the help of volunteers he completed the building within six months at a cost of around £5,000. 'The Anglo-Saxon Church in England was Orthodox,' Father Stephen expounds, 'so in becoming Orthodox we are returning to the root of our Christian faith.'

The saint to whom the church is dedicated was a 7th-century Irish prince and missionary. One of the Four Comely Saints – the other three winsome gents being Brendan of Birr, Conall and Berchán – Fursey sailed to England with two priests and his brothers, Foillan and Ultan (both also marked for sainthood), some time after 630. Crossing the country by Roman road they received a warm welcome from Sigeberht, King of the East Angles, who was already a Christian. The monarch gave the monk Cnobheresburg (probably Burgh Castle, a Roman fort near Great Yarmouth), which the latter transformed into a monastery. From this base the group converted many of the East Angles to Christianity. However, after 10 years or so, Fursey found himself called to preach the gospel to the Franks. He sailed across the channel and founded a new monastery at Lagny, near Paris. He died on the road, in about 650, at a place called Mézerolles.

Writing less than a hundred years later, the Venerable Bede remarked of the saint that he was 'renowned for his words and works, outstanding in goodness'. He recounts Fursey's habit of falling into

trances during which he saw heaven, hell and dystopian visions of the future on Earth. These visions came to have a great deal of influence on western European theology, the ideas expressed in Dante's *Divine Comedy* being a prime example.

There's something of the medieval saint about Father Stephen himself. Silver in beard, 6ft 4in tall and a self-styled walking miracle (ask him about the healing of his broken back), he's a larger-than-life character in a smaller-than-life setting.

The church he built is a Byzantine basilica in miniature, complete with high rows of tiny arched windows. Unapologetically shed-like from the outside – the only telltale sign being a small white cross at the eastern end of the roof – as soon as the narrow front door opens you know that you are entering a sacred space, for the sweet and heady scent of incense comes billowing out. Once inside, it is the eyes that are feted because, covering almost every available space on the walls, are icons. There are about 300, according to a devotee who took the trouble to count them. The pick of the bunch is a modern one depicting the missionary team: St Fursey, Foillan, Ultan and the two priests. Curiously, all five have almost exactly the same features, as if they were quintuplets. 'The Holy Icons are windows into heaven,' Father Stephen says in explanation of the

proliferation of icons, 'and by our prayerful life in the Church we experience their presence and prayer.'

The altar is separated from the nave by a partition on which there are large paintings of Christ and the Virgin Mary. Between these are what might be taken for the swing doors of a Wild West saloon if it weren't for the scenes from the lives of various saints painted upon them. There are also two slender side doors utilised when the congregation is processing. Their numbers can reach up to 18, packing the place out even when everyone stands, and making it necessary to use the garden for processions as well as the church.

The beautiful painted reliquary above the door contains a collection of Christian artefacts. Those coming in search of a sliver of the True Cross will be disappointed, but there are two primary relics: a piece of the skull of St Theodore, the Abbot of Croyland in Lincolnshire, who was slain by the Danes at the abbey altar in 869; and a section of the 'gospel oak' from Essex where St Cedd preached (see St Peter-on-the-Wall, p88, and St Andrew's, Greensted, p78). Secondary relics are stones from Iona and Holy Island, where saints once walked, and a piece of rock on which the Russian Saint Seraphim of Sarov knelt. They are venerated annually at the end of October and on the saints' feast days.

Now growing in number, the congregation is planning a new Orthodox basilica in the next-door town of Stalham. Fans of E F Schumacher's maxim that 'small is beautiful' will be relieved to learn that it will be only about twice the size of the current church, which would still make it one of the smallest in the country. 🗏

21 ST MARY'S
BARTON BENDISH

The glorious Norman doorway ranks among the finest in England.

SPIRITUAL ORIENTATION
Church of England (Churches Conservation Trust)

PHYSICAL ORIENTATION
Boughton Long Road, Barton Bendish, Downham Market, Norfolk PE33 9DN
Grid reference: TF 709 054
OS Landranger map 143

PUBLIC TRANSPORT
From Downham Market railway station (abelliogreateranglia.co.uk; 0345 6007245) it's a 10-minute walk into town to the bus station. The twice-daily (not Sunday) 62 bus (wnct.co.uk; 01553 776971) will convey you to Fincham from where it is a 2.5-mile walk (half of which is on the former Roman road and now rather busy A1122) to the church on the outskirts of Barton Bendish.

OPENING ARRANGEMENTS
Open daily from 10am to 5pm.

SERVICES
None.

here can be few churches in England in such a fortunate setting as this. Cradled on two sides by trees, St Mary's stands in a graveyard, the greater portion of which has surrendered to wild flowers (and, it has to be said, a fair few nettles).

Overcoming a disaster that could have all but finished it off, the church has managed to retain the simple charm with which its early 14th-century builders imbued it.

Nowadays, St Mary's finds itself a little removed from the heart of Barton Bendish, though this may not always have been the case, for in medieval times the village boasted three churches, suggesting that the community was once large and populous.

Built of flint and rubble, St Mary's has been rendered with lime to a light honeycomb finish that fairly glows in the sun. So much of the roof is covered with moss that it gives the impression that the church emerged fully formed from the earth like a giant toadstool. Indeed, it's easy not to notice that the roof is in fact thatched, as it almost certainly would have been when the church was built.

There was once a tower but this crashed dramatically to the ground during a storm in 1710, taking with it some of the west end of the nave. The church was not rebuilt until 1789, and then the £80 spent on it – equivalent to spending about £750,000 on a project today – did not run to replacing the tower or even re-establishing the nave at its former

length. However, much else was achieved, including the adding of a cupola for a bell in the west end, the reglazing of windows, the tiling of the floor – still in place today – the repair of the roof and the whitewashing of the walls. If those who carried out this last work were to come back today they would be impressed by the current blindingly white walls which are what first strikes the eye on entering, even before the box pews.

Most importantly, the £80 covered the cost of installing the elegant late Norman doorway which pre-dates the church. It came from the neighbouring All Saints, a church that was otherwise completely demolished the year before. It's tempting to speculate that the sudden desire to restore St Mary's after having left it so long a wreck was induced by the thought that this handsome doorway could quickly be found a new home. Still in excellent condition, the arch features a 'dog-tooth' motif from the late 12th century on the hood moulding (so called because it channels rain away). Inside this is a 'beakhead' design which, though relatively common in Norman doorways, is very rare for Norfolk. The innermost part of the arch is carved with rows of bobbins, while the shafts below it are decorated with leaves. The door itself, though of unknown date, retains its ancient closing ring.

A major restoration programme in 1865 is responsible for much of what we

see inside the church today. To a great extent the changes were made to conform with the exacting diktats for the design and decor of churches handed down by the Ecclesiological Movement, a campaign that wreaked so much havoc on ancient churches in the 19th century. The chancel was cleared of high pews; the pulpit and lectern were reduced in size; and a new communion rail was installed. The box pews were lowered and the seating was altered so that the entire congregation could face east, towards the altar. Several rows of hat pegs were also removed, an action that has all the hallmarks of an autocratic broom sweeping through.

The vestry doorway in the north side of the chancel has a 14th-century style arch with carved heads, one of a woman with a square headdress, the other of a

man with a plaited hairstyle typical in the late 1300s. Opposite is a door reserved for the priest. It's worth taking a wander outside to have a look at this doorway with its charming crocketed ogee arch and animal faces. While you're out there, note the windows on the south, east and west sides, which all sport tracery dating from the early 14th century. They're fashioned in the Decorated style and feature some particularly satisfying carved heads.

Back inside, the painting on the south wall of the nave is something of a mystery. The finer details have been lost to posterity so that all that can be made out is the outline of a figure standing inside a cartwheel that hovers above another figure on a double-handed bier. Pevsner posited that this mural, which was painted around 1330, might have shown some scene intended to keep parishioners on the straight and narrow. Moralistic medieval artists often used wheels to illustrate church teachings such as the Seven Deadly Sins and this could be one such, with the female figure symbolising Pride.

Certainly the bier below would suggest it served as some sort of memento mori, though mortality rates being what they were in the first half of the 14th century, a reminder of one's own loose grip on existence would hardly seem to have been necessary. The fact that the figure is shown on a cartwheel has also led to the (probably erroneous) belief that this is a painting of Catherine of Alexandria, the saint famously sentenced to execution on a spiked wheel (the wheel reputedly shattered so she was beheaded instead) and whose name lives on in the Catherine wheels set alight on firework nights.

There are eight pieces of furniture that warrant investigation. Four of these are the rustic pews that reside towards the back, one of which bears the date 1637. The font, with its hexagonal bowl, is carved in an appropriately 14th-century style, though it actually dates to the mid-19th century when it was given to the church by one Lady Berney. In the east wall you'll find a recess, known as an aumbry. This is medieval and was used to store holy oils or the plate, bread and wine used in Communion. Finally, the *pièce de résistance* is the Carolean altar table that bears the legend 'EL 1633' and perfectly mirrors the artful simplicity of the church architecture.

In the sanctuary floor lies the black ledger slab of Simon, Mary and Sarah Tiffin. This sports an octopus, an 18th-century symbol of immortality. Sadly, the church itself proved far from immortal, being declared redundant in 1974. It was taken on by the Churches Conservation Trust (then known as the Redundant Churches Fund) and it is to this organisation's great credit that this aesthetically pleasing church is preserved for us all to enjoy. 🪶

GUYHIRN CHAPEL
GUYHIRN

The chapel's glory comes from the fact that its constituent parts work together to form a satisfying whole.

SPIRITUAL ORIENTATION
Puritan then Church of England (Churches Conservation Trust)

PHYSICAL ORIENTATION
High Road, Guyhirn, Wisbech, Cambridgeshire PE13 4ED
Grid reference: TF 403 040
OS Landranger map 143

PUBLIC TRANSPORT
From March railway station (abelliogreateranglia.co.uk; 0345 6007245) head south through the town to Gull Road. Take the 46 bus (norfolkgreen.co.uk; 01553 776980) to Guyhirn and walk up High Road to the church.

OPENING ARRANGEMENTS
'Often open.' If it is closed, the key for the church is kept at the house by the fruit and veg stall on the High Road. With your back to the church, turn right along the road and you'll find the house on your right. Alternatively, call 01945 410755.

SERVICES
There are two services a year. A Thanksgiving service in July celebrates the 1975 restoration of the building and an Epiphany service is held in January.

If you want a taste of what religious life was like under the Puritans, you could hardly do better than to visit Guyhirn Chapel. An exceedingly fine example of a Puritan house of worship, Guyhirn's features are nearly all either original or painstakingly crafted replicas, so what you see is almost precisely what the first worshippers would have experienced three and a half centuries ago, with the possible exception of a gallery which, if it did exist, no longer does. As the physical embodiment of their extreme Calvinist beliefs, the chapel is flawless.

Although Cromwell was in good health when a sum of money was given for the building of Guyhirn Chapel, when it was finished almost a decade later he had been dead two years. Calamitously for the brand new congregation, the restitution of the monarchy occurred in the very same year that they held their first service there. It makes this building even more remarkable because it promulgated a form of Christianity that, even as it opened its doors, was falling dramatically from favour and would, two years later, become outlawed altogether. Perhaps even more extraordinarily, aside from the addition of

a communion rail and a flue for a fire (both since removed), the chapel was untouched by the triumphant returning Stuarts and the tirelessly interfering Victorians. They even seem to have forgotten to consecrate the church. The practice had been shelved during the Commonwealth and there is no record of such a service having been carried out subsequently.

Located alongside what was once a trackway leading from Peterborough to Wisbech, the chapel has north and west walls made of brick and rubble, while its south and east walls are constructed from Barnack stone, probably scavenged from nearby Thorney Abbey. In keeping with the Calvinist devotion to simplicity, the chapel is a straightforward rectangle fitted with five plain-glass mullioned windows, one of which is rather higher than the rest,

suggesting there was probably a gallery within. The chapel has a roof of red pantiles, which, although modern, is also likely to have been the covering chosen by the builders. The delicate bell-cote that sits on top of it is a faithful copy of the original which was found to be beyond repair during the 1975 restoration. The bell itself is from 1637, pre-dating the church.

Above the door a stone records the momentous year the church was finished – 1660 – and the initials RP. This latter inscription has caused historians some head-scratching, but it may refer to Richard Pettigrew, a steward of the Bedford Estate at Thorney. He was a known Puritan and may have been instrumental in having the chapel built.

Unlocking the door with the large and satisfyingly heavy key, the visitor enters the Cromwellian Puritan mind. Their

Talibanesque proscriptions included a blanket ban on sporting activities and entertainments, almost all works of art, all festivals (including Christmas), most forms of comfort, and even kneeling in church, which apparently had a whiff of Popery about it. They believed in the primacy of the Bible and the efficacy of long sermons and protracted prayers. They were not people who suspected Jesus of having a sense of humour. The interior reflects such attitudes, both in what is there and what has been omitted.

The walls are devoid of any adornment save the two rows of hat pegs, their extreme length an indicator of the lofty headgear then in use. The floors are of vernacular handmade bricks. The pews

– all of which are original except for the front four on the right – are high, straight-backed and narrow. Slouching was not an option and they are so tightly packed that there was no chance of kneeling either. Originally, the pulpit would have dominated the chapel to emphasise the pre-eminence of the 'pure word of God'. Regrettably, what has survived is but a section of the original pulpit, though it remains the highest piece of furniture in the chapel. The only elements that might be said to beautify the church are the Regency-style ventilators in the ceiling, but even these are far from showy. Now, as then, there is neither lighting nor heating.

A communion rail was installed at a later date when the church was Anglicanised. This would no doubt have sent shivers down the spines of the earlier congregants (for such a rail involved not simply kneeling but kneeling before a priest) and their shades will rejoice in the knowledge that it has been removed. The communion table is sadly not original but is reassuringly plain.

After the restitution of the monarchy, the church was incorporated into the Anglican church and kept open as a Chapel of Ease, so called because it spared the people of Guyhirn a 3-mile walk to the parish church at Wisbech St Mary. However, it appears that some elements of Calvinism lived on in the chapel, despite the harsh sentences that could in those times be visited upon dissenters. In 1685 the congregation was ordered to 'provide a surplice for your minister' (the donning of which demonstrated that the wearer was doctrinally orthodox). Presumably, the clergyman at Guyhirn was still kitted out in the traditional Puritan black gown.

The Chapel of Ease continued in regular use until 1878, when Guyhirn was provided with a new parish church. St Mary Magdalene (now closed) was designed and built by the eminent Gothic Revival architect George Gilbert Scott. The chapel at Guyhirn struggled on for 20 years offering monthly services but was eventually assigned a new role as a mortuary chapel. Despite occasional repairs, the building went into a seemingly irreversible decline and, after a final service on Sunday 5 November 1960 – 300 years after it had opened – the chapel was declared unsafe and closed.

It is due to the Churches Conservation Trust and the Rev Donald Dickinson, founder in 1973 of the Friends of Guyhirn Chapel of Ease, that the building was saved from demolition. The latter organisation's first president was none other than then Poet Laureate Sir John Betjeman, who was moved to write a few lines of doggerel about the chapel. The stanza is on display inside, in all its glory. What the Puritans would have made of the exhibition of poetry within the chapel is only too imaginable.

ST JOHN'S
LITTLE GIDDING

The austere beauty of the church is complemented by (literally) embroidered quotations from those who have found inspiration there.

SPIRITUAL ORIENTATION
Church of England

PHYSICAL ORIENTATION
Little Gidding, Huntingdon, Cambridgeshire PE28 5RJ
Grid reference: TL 127 816
OS Landranger map 142

PUBLIC TRANSPORT
From Huntingdon railway station (abelliogreateranglia.co.uk; 0345 6007245), a 46A bus (hact-cambs.co.uk; 01480 411114) will only get you as far as Alconbury Weston, a village famed for its fine floodwater culvert but still sadly 5 miles shy of the church. However, the National Cycle Network Route 12 will take you the whole 11 miles from Huntingdon railway station to the Little Gidding turn-off.

OPENING ARRANGEMENTS
Open daily. If the church is locked, find a warden of Ferrar House (the building nearest the church, which holds an exhibition about the Ferrar community) or ring Michael Keck (01832 293357).

For further information see littlegidding.org.uk and ferrarhouse.co.uk.

SERVICES
Noon 2nd Friday (Holy Communion)
These services are followed by lunch which can be booked by ringing Richard Scott (01480 890286) in advance. There are also five Evensong services held throughout the year and a 10.30am Eucharist on the Saturday closest to the Feast Day of Nicholas Ferrar (4 December).

ome churches have a single collision with history. St John's at Little Gidding has managed no fewer than three. It became the centre of a famous religious community, harboured a fleeing Charles I, and inspired one of the best-known poetic works of the 20th century.

Brick-built, with a dour off-white stone façade in the shape of a rocket, the church sits in a generous swathe of lawn surrounded by trees. Far from the nearest road, and tucked behind a large retreat house, the church is bathed in an aura of serenity and stillness.

Nothing but the foundations survive of the original church, which was given to the Order of the Knights Templars in 1185 by Maud Engaine. In 1312, the order was dissolved in England and St John's fell into the hands of the Knights Hospitaller, from whom St John Ambulance emerged. This confluence of St Johns is a coincidence: the Hospitallers' John is John the Baptist

while the church is dedicated to John the Divine, author of the Book of Revelation.

Nicholas Ferrar was a failed London merchant whose widowed mother Mary bought him the dilapidated manor at Little Gidding in order that he and his family had somewhere to live. They arrived in 1625 to find that St John's had fallen from grace and was being used as a barn. Mary insisted that the church be rebuilt from its very foundations before even the house

was renovated. More family members arrived, servants were hired, Nicholas was ordained a deacon, and a religious community of around 40 people was formed, following a pattern of work, prayer and teaching that fell somewhere between Protestantism and Catholicism. Ferrar also devised what he called a Harmony – literally cutting out lines from all four gospels with scissors and sticking them into a book so that they formed a

continuous narrative. Charles I was a fan and further handmade copies were ordered by members of the royal family and celebrities of the day. The community was not, as is often reported, ransacked by Cromwellian forces in 1646 enraged at its 'popery', though many of the family did escape to Holland for a few years in 1643.

Charles visited on three occasions, the last under somewhat stressful circumstances. With the Battle of Naseby lost, the monarch fled Oxford for the safety of Scotland and on 2 May 1646 came to Little Gidding, a Royalist-sympathising oasis in Parliamentary-supporting Huntingdonshire. Nicholas Ferrar had died nine years earlier so the king was received by John Ferrar, who, fearing that the manor would not prove a safe hiding place, led the monarch across the fields to Coppingford Lodge under cover of darkness.

There's a certain darkness inside the church too. This is down to a later John Ferrar who, with his son Thomas, refurbished St John's in 1714, installing dark wooden panelling on the walls and ceiling that gives the nave a tunnel-like appearance. The two men were also responsible for the façade and for reducing the length of the church by 2ft.

Rather than pews or seats, stalls line the walls so that congregants face each other across the stone floor of the nave. Though the stalls have the feel of the Knights of the Round Table, or at the very least some fancy order of monks, they were actually installed in 1853 by William Hopkinson, who had bought the estate and restored the church. A copy of an engraving made in 1851 shows St John's immediately before his intervention and, it has to be said, he didn't do a bad job.

The walls are decorated with austere cross-stitch embroideries bearing somewhat stern messages. One quotes the words Nicholas Ferrar is said to have uttered on his deathbed, while a poem called 'Bitter-Sweet' by poet and Anglican priest George Herbert, a friend of Ferrar's, strikes a gentler note:

Ah my dear angry Lord,
Since though dost love, yet strike;
Cast down, yet help afford;
Sure I will do the like.
I will complain, yet praise;

I will bewail, approve;
And all my sour-sweet days
I will lament, and love.

The plain glass Venetian window in the chancel is from 1980. The previous window, depicting the Crucifixion, was too large to support the wall into which it was built and had to be removed. Nearby, a small circle of stained glass quotes Charles I's words to Nicholas Ferrar after a visit: 'It is the right, good, old way you are in; keep in it.' Ferrar's body lies outside the church door in a simple table tomb.

T S Eliot visited the church on 25 May 1936, having had an interest in Christian communities sparked by reading biographies of Nicholas Ferrar. The experience led to his writing of the *Four Quartets*, one of which he titled 'Little Gidding'. A meditation on time and timeless moments, it came out in stages over 1941–42 and was the last thing Eliot published before his death 23 years later. One of the embroideries in the church quotes some lines from the Little Gidding section.

Now serving as a chapel of ease, though with only occasional services, this is truly a church like no other. If you are visiting for the first time, go in late spring to see the ornamental cherry by the entrance – a mass of pink that softens the space-age-mausoleum-face through which St John's looks out on the world.

ALL SAINTS
SHORTHAMPTON

The vast array of cathedral-standard medieval wall paintings is a wonder to behold.

SPIRITUAL ORIENTATION
Church of England

PHYSICAL ORIENTATION
Shorthampton, Oxfordshire OX7 3HW
Grid reference: SP 328 201
OS Landranger map 164

PUBLIC TRANSPORT
There's no bus service from Charlbury railway station (gwr.com; 0345 7000125). It's a little under 2 miles to the church, first taking the B4437, then a right turn up Catsham Lane and a left into Shorthampton.

OPENING ARRANGEMENTS
Open daily.

SERVICES
3pm 2nd Sunday (November to March) Evening Prayer
6pm 2nd Sunday (April to October) Evening Prayer
Additional services Ash Wednesday, Easter, Pentecost, All Saints and Christmas
For further details see charlburychurch.co.uk.

owever long you have set aside to look around this little church in the Cotswolds, it's a good idea to double or perhaps treble it, for inside you'll find not just one or two medieval paintings but a whole gallery of them.

From the outside, there is nothing particular about the pleasant-looking if slightly boxy little building that hints at the wonders within. If anything, it is the setting that is more suggestive. It's not dissimilar to that which would have greeted late medieval visitors: Shorthampton's few houses clustered

around a chapel surrounded by agricultural land with a view of yet more farmland draping itself across the shallow Evenlode Valley.

Many medieval wall paintings in British churches were destroyed either during the Reformation or, later, by the Puritans. How the murals in this church escaped the depredations of both those movements is unclear, though there is some evidence that the images were covered up by high box pews and panelling in the 16th or 17th century. The paintings were restored to as much of their former glory as was possible in 1903, when repairs made to the church led to their discovery.

The church was founded at some point in the 12th century. Back then it was even smaller than it is today and may have consisted of a mere nave. The roof would have been thatched, with the walls rendered and painted white, presenting a very different face to the creamy-beige exposed Cotswold stone now on display. The present chancel arch is from the 14th century, so a chancel must have been added no later than this. It has a significantly lower roof than the nave and a rather endearing little window in the south wall that adds an air of domesticity. Then, as now, there was no tower, though there is a rather jaunty bell-cote at the eastern end of the nave roof, its two bells open to the elements.

The mystery of why there is a huge, rather clumsy-looking hole (or 'squint') in the chancel arch is solved when you discover that in the 15th century the south wall of the nave was shifted outwards 6ft to accommodate a new altar in that part of the church. The squint was made so that the congregation in this freshly created space could see the chancel altar and the priest officiating there.

For a feel of how the 12th-century church appeared, look for the round-headed window in the north wall, the blocked door in the same wall, the 'tub' font (so called because it sits, rather unglamorously, on the floor) and another blocked door high up in the west wall. Difficult though it may be to believe, this last was probably the original entrance to the chapel and was moved from ground level on the north wall in the 18th century to serve a gallery, since removed.

The box pews are from the 1700s, very comfortably upholstered and noticeably more exclusive on the pulpit side of the church, where they are built up far higher than those on the other side of the aisle.

However, it is possible that you will have noticed none of these details because your attention has been monopolised by the riot of soft reds and ochres on the walls. There are so many paintings that only a brief résumé can be attempted here. Happily, they are covered in detail by an inexpensive guide sold in the church.

The painting in the squint illustrates a story told in the non-biblical Gospel of St Thomas and includes a rare sighting of one of the Messiah's siblings. The five-year-old Jesus is shown fashioning some birds out of mud. When Joseph tells him off for doing this 'work' on the Sabbath, Jesus orders the birds to fly. They do so, singing out their praises to God.

To the right of this, the backdrop to the (missing) lesser altar looks like a single work but was actually painted at two distinct times. The earlier one shows Christ's sweat falling as drops of blood, as is reported to have occurred in the Garden of Gethsemane before his arrest. Perhaps this image was felt to be too downbeat because a second was added, depicting the traditional 'Christ in Majesty'.

The epic artwork sprawled over the chancel arch, which is now rather difficult to make out, was apparently an artist's impression of the Day of Judgement.

On the north wall you will find an unidentified archbishop (possibly St Edmund of Abingdon) and St Frideswide, the patron saint of Oxford University. There's a certain irony in that, as a woman, she would have been barred from matriculating there until 1920.

One of the best preserved and most detailed paintings can be found in the reveal of the south window. Here stands St Zita, the patron saint of domestic servants (see the Church of the Good Shepherd, Lullington, p70). St Loy, patron saint of blacksmiths, stands to the left of the entrance; while on the west wall there is an intriguing fragment of a dragon's wing. Meanwhile, a cartouche of King Solomon's Prayer is from the 18th century, when godly text was favoured over the idolatrous image.

The subjects for the earlier works would have been chosen by monks from the priory at Eynsham, who held sway over the parish. Their decision to portray Jesus in a family setting alongside a line-up of practical contemplative saints with whom the 15th-century congregation would have identified gives the church a friendly, gentle and human feel. You get the feeling that the Day of Judgement was only painted in order to satisfy any passing bishop that there was at least a whiff of brimstone about the place... 🥀

ST OSWALD'S
WIDFORD

The 14th-century wall paintings in the chancel are a delight to the eye, even if it's hard to tell quite what's going on.

SPIRITUAL ORIENTATION

Church of England

PHYSICAL ORIENTATION

Widford, nr Burford, Oxfordshire OX18 4DU
Grid reference: SP 273 120
OS Landranger map 163

PUBLIC TRANSPORT

Although Ascott-under-Wychwood (6 miles) is the closest railway station, it's easier, though by no means speedy, to get to Widford by bus from Oxford (various train operators). From Frideswide Square (stop R9), take the S1 bus (stagecoachbus.com; 01865 772250) to the bus garage in Witney from where the V21 bus (villagerbus.com; 01451 832114) will convey you to the Swan Inn at Swinbrook. From there it's a very pleasant walk through the village, left along the road just before the remarkable St Mary's church (also well worth a look around – various members of the Mitford family are buried in the churchyard) and across the fields on a footpath to St Oswald's – a stroll of just over half a mile in all.

OPENING ARRANGEMENTS

Open daily.

SERVICES

6pm 4th Sunday (Evening Prayer).

There are many churches in England that share their foundations with buildings constructed by Normans or even Saxons. Only a select few can trace their roots back all the way to the Romano-British and St Oswald's is one of them (see also St Peter-on-the-Wall, p88). Alone in an open field, permanently besieged by cattle, the little church stands proudly on the footings of a Roman villa. Look past the doomed livestock and virtually all you will see in every direction is trees and fields, for this is Oxfordshire's lovely yet little-known Windrush Valley.

The current church is almost entirely 13th century, though it has a few earlier features and was once part of a village that has vanished but for a few lumps and bumps. It was established by the monks of St Oswald's Priory in Gloucestershire, a religious community founded by Ethelfleda, the daughter of King Alfred. They oversaw it right up until Henry VIII brought about the Dissolution of the Monasteries.

Curiously, Widford was a little exclave of Gloucestershire until 1844 when logic prevailed and it was subsumed into Oxfordshire. Given the scattered

population in these parts, it's remarkable that the church remained open until 1859. Used as a barn, it quickly deteriorated and, had the Society for the Protection of Ancient Buildings not stepped in at the turn of that century, the church would almost certainly have been lost. In 1904, they struck lucky and discovered the medieval wall paintings and the mosaic floor that lies beneath the patchwork of sandy-coloured flagstones. Until fairly recently, parts of the mosaic were on show but they have had to be covered again to deter thieves.

The walk across the field from the lane gives ample opportunity to admire the exterior of the church, built of local limestone and roofed with stone slates.

A single roof runs the length of the nave and chancel and has a bell-cote straddling it like a jockey. As you approach up the slope, trefoiled lancet windows become visible. These contrast in date and style with the large oblong west window which is a late addition but gives the church something of the look of a handsome manor house, at least from below.

In the churchyard, protected from farm animals by a sturdy dry-stone wall, the bright yellows of cowslips and dandelions add some cheer to the headstones and grave-slabs (including one decorated with a prodigious sword). Step inside and it's difficult not to feel a warmth towards this church because it's such a comfortable little place with its pastel pink

walls, worn flagstone floor, exposed-beam roof, miniature Georgian box pews and, hunkered down in a corner, a desk suitable for only the slenderest of parish clerks and a pulpit knocked together from the panels of a screen. Both the nave and the chancel are cosy spaces, being divided from one another by a wall pierced only by a low arch. Even the two large boards that bark out the Ten Commandments have such a graceful quality to them that their bite is somewhat neutralised.

Just inside the door, what looks to be a badly broken tray resting on a sawn-off pillar is actually a 13th-century tub font and lid. On the wall opposite, a 15th-century St Christopher is partly painted over by a 17th-century royal coat of arms.

Pass through to the chancel and you'll find a piscina with a trefoiled head. This recess has become something of a bone of contention. The official church guide claims it's Early English (1189–1280), while Pevsner has it down as Perp (i.e. Perpendicular – 1377–1547). A 13th-century dating seems the more likely. The altar rail causes fewer problems, being unquestionably Jacobean. However, it is the wall paintings – from around 1340 – that really catch the eye. On the north wall, in the upper section, we see St Lawrence being martyred (St Edmund may also make an appearance, but this is another area of dispute). Underneath there is a depiction of the Three Living Kings

and the Three Dead Kings. This is a medieval morality tale, the crux being, 'As you are, so were we: and as we are, so you will be.' Other unidentified figures can be seen in the reveals of the lancet window. Opposite them is a painting in less happy condition and its subjects are difficult to pin down, though the lower portion may show St Martin of Tours gallantly giving half his cloak to a poor naked man.

If there ever was a study of Oswald on these walls, it is lost now. The saint to whom the church is dedicated was born around 605, a younger brother of King (and later St) Edwin of Northumbria. Converted at Iona while in exile in Scotland, he was proclaimed King of Northumbria when Edwin was killed in battle. He went on to defeat one of his brother's nemeses, Cadwallon of Gwynedd, before dying in battle in 642 at the hands of the other, Penda of Mercia, that great slayer of saints. While Oswald's head eventually ended up at Durham Cathedral in St Cuthbert's coffin (probably best not to ask), tradition has it that the rest of his dismembered body spent a night in this church on its way to St Oswald's Priory. Sadly, that's almost certainly untrue. Firstly, Widford has never been on the way to anywhere and, secondly, Oswald's bones appear to have been doled out around the north of England to be squirrelled away in reliquaries. Who'd be a saint, eh? ▨

ST MARY OF THE ANGELS
BROWNSHILL

The Romanesque-influenced Arts and Crafts interior is a real delight.

SPIRITUAL ORIENTATION
Roman Catholic (Friends of Friendless Churches)

PHYSICAL ORIENTATION
St Mary's Way, Brownshill, Stroud, Gloucestershire GL6 8AW
Grid reference: SO 883 025
OS Landranger map 162

PUBLIC TRANSPORT
From Stroud railway station (gwr.com; 0345 7000125) it's a very short walk to Rowcroft, from where you can take the no. 64 bus (stagecoachbus.com; 01452 418630) to Lewiston Mill on the Toadsmoor Road. From there, it's just over half a mile by way of an occasionally steep footpath up Blackness to the chapel.

OPENING ARRANGEMENTS
Kept locked. Contact the office of Friends of Friendless Churches (020 7236 3934) for details of the keyholder.

SERVICES
None.

O n the side of a hill, enjoying sweeping views of the Toadsmoor Valley, St Mary's of the Angels is not only the last remnant of a short-lived and ill-fated religious community but also a shining example of 20th-century church design. Built in the Romanesque style with an Arts and Crafts interior, it was the work of two men: the acclaimed architect W D Caröe and Douglas Strachan, who is often reckoned to be the finest stained-glass artist Scotland has ever produced.

Brownshill, a maze of narrow winding lanes, is a small village that began life as a weavers' squatter settlement. Its most remarkable building by some margin is this little Catholic chapel founded by Bertha Kessler and Katherine Hudson. The two women paid the price for their work with the First Aid Nursing Auxiliary in World War I with recurring spells of psychiatric illness. After meeting inspirational Congregationalist minister W E Orchard, they dedicated themselves to the healing of others.

In 1927 they bought a house in Brownshill (next to where St Mary's now stands) called Tanglewood, rechristened it Templewood, and founded a little community treating female psychiatric patients. When, in 1934, they were received into the Catholic Church, the Bishop of Clifton encouraged them to build their own chapel, since there was none in the village. They scraped together £2,000 of their own money, which was little enough even then, and boldly approached William Caröe, who at 73 was in the twilight of a long and illustrious career that encompassed the building of more than 30 churches. With nothing to prove, he designed a church that, though principally in the Romanesque style beloved of the Normans, also had a Byzantine apse (he had lately built a church in Cyprus) and a gallery that owed more to Sweden than merrie olde England, though he himself was of Danish heritage. Despite being a '20th-century Norman' church, it can actually claim some ancient ecclesiastical roots, having been built on the site of a barn constructed from the stones of a Saxon church. If your eyesight (and imagination) is very acute, you may just about make out, in the adjacent spinney, the mound which is all that remains of St Mary's predecessor.

Congregation of the Servants of the Paraclete, whose mission was to help priests with psychiatric problems. The two communities merged and changed name again but began to decline – the last remaining nuns left Brownshill in 2006 (the private residence opposite still bears the name 'St Mary's Convent').

Constructed of local limestone, the church sports a large shingled wooden bell-cote on its Cotswold stone and slate roof. In its shadow, the churchyard hosts a smattering of identical wooden crosses of the simplest possible design. They mark the last resting places of Bertha Kessler and Katherine Hudson – who died within three weeks of one another in 1963 – along with nuns, monks, clergymen and others with connections to the community.

From the road that runs above it, St Mary's looks larger than it actually is – a quirk that becomes apparent as soon as you walk into it. The interior is inspired by William Morris' Arts and Crafts Movement and its concrete barrel vaulting gives the sense of being in a tunnel. At the west end a timber gallery (currently inaccessible) has a gossamer lightness to it that is magnified by the solidity and sheer weight of the walls and roof that surround it.

Kessler and Hudson's church was begun in 1930 and finally consecrated seven years later. Caröe died the following year. The community became the Templewood Home of Rest and began accepting male patients as other houses in the village were purchased for the cause. By 1951, Kessler and Hudson established a Tertiary Chapter of the Dominican Order. Eight years later they were joined in the village by an American order called the

Walk down the aisle, between pews whose subtly undulating backs have something of a calm sea about them, and you'll pass the door of a spacious vestry and go under a grand Romanesque arch

that divides the nave from the apse. This latter space is dominated by a bare altar of pure white stone.

St Mary's is surprisingly rich in natural light, which is certainly not a feature of genuine Norman churches. The reason for this is that, along with the thoroughly Norman-style lancets in the apse, larger round-arched windows run the length of the nave. All the glasswork was designed by Douglas Strachan, who was also responsible for the windows of the Scottish National War Memorial and St Margaret's Chapel (p267), both in Edinburgh Castle. The lancets commemorate Katherine, Bertha and Bertha's brother, who was a generous supporter of his sister's work.

Despite being located in an insignificant Gloucestershire village, the Templewood community attracted many illustrious visitors, including Mother Teresa of Calcutta and Spitfire pilot Douglas Bader, whose exploits were recreated by Kenneth More in the film *Reach for the Sky*. Tragically, the house was destroyed when a Lancaster bomber crashed into it in 1946. The crew was killed but fortunately there were no fatalities on the ground.

The church came into the care of the Friends of Friendless Churches in 2011, though in this particular case the charity's name is an inopportune one. Such was their love for St Mary's that, in order to save the church, the local villagers raised the money to buy it so that they could hand it to the organisation for safe-keeping. It stands today as a tribute to the work of two devoted friends and two highly accomplished craftsmen. 🦋

27 ODDA'S CHAPEL
DEERHURST

The all-but-windowless walls of the nave instantly sweep visitors back to the last days of the Saxons.

SPIRITUAL ORIENTATION
Roman Catholic (English Heritage)

PHYSICAL ORIENTATION
Deerhurst, Gloucestershire GL19 4BX
Grid reference: SO 869 298
OS Landranger map 150

PUBLIC TRANSPORT
From Cheltenham railway station (various train operators) walk to Clarence Street (stop 9) to take the 42A bus (stagecoachbus.com; 01452 418630) to Highfield Trading Estate on the A38. It's a 1.75-mile walk, taking the B4213 opposite, the first right to Deerhurst, then following the signs to the chapel.

OPENING ARRANGEMENTS
10am–6pm daily (late March to October)
10am–4pm daily (November to late March)
No admission is charged.

SERVICES
None.

But for two chance discoveries 200 years apart and a nifty piece of detective work by a real life Father Brown, we would not be aware of the existence of this fantastically well-preserved Saxon chapel tucked away in a somnolent backwater of the Severn Valley. The story of its discovery is almost as remarkable as the church itself.

The sense that there's a tale to tell here is obvious as soon as you arrive, for there's something undeniably odd about Odda's Chapel. Why, for instance, is a stone Saxon church attached to an exquisite black-and-white timber-framed house? Looking inside, we come across two further puzzling eccentricities: the outline of a bricked-up fireplace and some ancient beams crossing the chancel a little above head height. And does the stone with a Latin inscription contain a clue or muddy the waters further?

Despite these various enigmas, the church is a surprisingly simple one. It consists of a nave and chancel divided by an arch, with a doorway in the north wall. It also used to possess a door opposite the entrance but that has since been blocked up. The nave is lit by two high windows facing each other – look up at the one on the south side and you can still see its frame of good Saxon oak. Their smallness has the effect of making the already impressively lofty walls tower even higher above the visitor. Aside from portions that have been restored in brick, these are built of blue lias stone from a nearby quarry.

The chapel is all but empty save for benches along three walls of the nave and a stone device in a corner holding a little bouquet of dried flowers. The decision to keep it uncluttered has made it a tranquil place, where you feel the very walls would soak up your troubles if they could.

Yet it would never have been identified as a place of worship had it not been for two providential discoveries and the Rev George Butterworth's resolve to turn detective. The vicar of Deerhurst had become intrigued by the Odda Stone, an ancient artefact unearthed by Sir John Powell in 1675 in an orchard close to the local parish church. It was inscribed in Latin, a translation of which reads:

Earl Odda ordered this royal hall to be built and dedicated in honour of the Holy Trinity for the soul of his brother Aelfric, taken up [into heaven] from this place. Ealdred was the bishop who dedicated the building on the second of the Ides of April in the fourteenth year of the reign of Edward, king of the English.

This particular Edward was Edward the Confessor. He reigned from 1042 to that most memorable of dates, 1066. We can therefore deduce that the dedication of the chapel took place on 12 April 1056 (the Ides of April occur on the 13th – 'the second of' in this context referring to the day before). Earl Odda was a relative of the king's and at one time responsible for the governorship of much of southwest England. The Aelfric in question died three years before the chapel was built, while Odda himself enjoyed the chapel for only four months before he too died.

The local parish church (also well worth a visit) was once part of Deerhurst Priory and happens to be Anglo-Saxon. It would have been most convenient had this been the royal hall alluded to on the stone. However, that church is very early Saxon, probably dating back to the 7th century, so could not have been the mystery chapel.

Butterworth turned to the medieval chronicle of Tewkesbury Abbey, where he came across a description of a church dedicated to the Holy Trinity. The writer located it opposite the entrance to Deerhurst Priory. The breakthrough came

+ODDA DVX IVSSIT hNC
REGIAM AVIAM CONSTRVI
ATQVE DE DⒶRIINHONO
Rⓔ ŠTRINITATISPROANIMAⒺR
MANISVIÆLFRICIⓋⒺDEHOC
LOⒸASVPTAⒺALDREDVSVERO
ⒺPS QVIEANDⒺ ⒹDCAVITIIID
BVS APLXIIIIAVEANNOSREG
NIⒺADWARDIREGISANGLORV

This is an exact copy of
a stone found here A.D.1675
and preserved at Oxford.

in 1885 when repairs were made to a house called Abbots Court in Deerhurst. The good reverend had long since harboured suspicions that one wing of the great house was ancient owing to the extreme thickness of the walls. He stripped away a section of the plaster and found himself looking at a rounded arch. Tearing away more plaster he discovered an inscription on a stone that was set in a 16th-century chimney-stack. It was not whole but, almost beyond a doubt, it read, 'This altar has been dedicated in honour of the Holy Trinity'. The chapel built to honour Earl Odda's late brother had been found.

Its attachment to the half-timbered house can be explained by the fact that Earl Odda would have appended it to his own lodgings. After the Dissolution of the Monasteries the owners of Odda's former house found a cheap way to enlarge their property by incorporating the long-abandoned chapel into it.

The story of Odda's Chapel has striking parallels with that of St Laurence's Church in Bradford-on-Avon (p34): they are both late Saxon churches, they both 'disappeared' for several centuries, and their existence was brought to light again by a clergyman (a canon clearly outranks a vicar, so St Laurence's won on that score). However, whereas St Laurence's became a school and a warehouse during its time in purgatory, Odda's Chapel, as far as we know, was only ever used as part of a home. The chancel was made into a bedroom – those beams that fly across it transformed the upper part into a second-storey room – while the nave became a kitchen, which explains the presence of the fireplace (clearly visible behind the west bench). The windows in the chancel were added to make it more habitable.

Below those windows a replica of the Odda Stone has been set into the wall. The stone itself is in the Ashmolean Museum in Oxford. It's our good fortune that the riddle it posed for two centuries has now been solved and the answer stands revealed for all to see. 🪶

28 ALL SAINTS
BILLESLEY

Two pieces of exquisitely carved stone, one of which includes artwork from late Anglo-Saxon times, make a visit here particularly rewarding.

SPIRITUAL ORIENTATION

Formerly an estate church (Churches Conservation Trust)

PHYSICAL ORIENTATION

Billesley, Stratford-upon-Avon, Warwickshire B49 6NF
Grid reference: SP 148 568
OS Landranger map 151

PUBLIC TRANSPORT

From Wilmcote railway station (londonmidland.com; chilternrailways.co.uk) it's a 2.5-mile cycle ride or walk. Alternatively, from Stratford-upon-Avon (same companies) take the 26 bus (stagecoachbus.com; 01788 535555) and alight at the stop nearest the Billesley turn-off and stroll the short distance to the Billesley Manor Hotel. On arrival, walk up the hotel driveway. Pass the entrances to the car park and follow a 'Historic Church' signpost on the right-hand side that guides visitors along a path to the church. Anyone driving in will need to visit the hotel reception afterwards to obtain the code to raise the exit barrier.

OPENING ARRANGEMENTS

Open daily.

SERVICES

None.

on't let All Saints Church fool you. As you walk towards it you'll see an information board to your right full of fascinating facts about the lost village of Billesley Trussell. Humps and bumps in the field before you seem to be all that is left of the once-thriving township, a place visited so often by the twin scourges of the Black Death and poor harvests that by 1428 the population had dwindled to just four. Glance to your left at the church and, even though it's partially obscured by trees, it's manifestly evident that it dates from Georgian times and so couldn't possibly have been the parish church of the ill-starred village.

Or so it would appear. However, amble up the delightful avenue of lime trees to the church and you may hear a faint chuckle coming from beneath the floor of the sanctuary. Buried there, along with his wife Lucy, is Bernard Whalley, the man whose extensive remodelling in 1692 transformed the building from a parish church long since stripped of its parish into a classical-looking adornment to the manor, which by then was its only neighbour.

The clues are there if you look closely. Examine the wall below the nave windows at either side of the transept and you'll see masonry laid in the herringbone style of the 11th or early 12th century. There's a blocked Gothic doorway in the north wall and two excellent pieces of 12th-century carved stone now proudly displayed in the transept.

Billesley Trussell was a Saxon settlement that was clearly doing well for itself by the time the men from the Domesday Book came calling. By the middle of the 12th century it had become necessary to add a north aisle to the church – built of local lias stone rubble – while a magnificent tympanum over a doorway, followed later on by new Gothic windows, would have impressed upon visitors the importance of the community. It was only after the 1330s that the village's fortunes took a downturn – the effect of the plague and meagre harvests being exacerbated by intensive sheep farming. The north aisle was demolished and by the time Bernard Whalley took the church in hand it seems to have been well on the way to ruination.

However, this state of affairs hasn't dented the church's claim to have been the wedding venue of William Shakespeare and Anne Hathaway. Unfortunately, there are no parish records available to verify this, but it is known that Shakespeare's granddaughter Elizabeth Nash married her second husband here on 5 June 1649. She lived some distance away and had no other discernible ties to the church so it's possible that she chose it because of an association with her famous grandfather.

Forty years later, Whalley bought the manor and after about three years turned his attentions to the dilapidated church on its doorstep. The overhaul was so extensive that almost everywhere you look you'll see Whalley's fingerprints – even the

unusual Romanesque apse was largely rebuilt by the new squire. The two most obvious examples of his work are the new doorway, which now serves as an entrance, and the transept in the south wall. The doorway was built at the west end so that it faced the manor (now a hotel), which had been moved from its original moated position in the village. The transept probably accommodated Whalley's private pew. The large grey sandstone doorway that granted access to it via the west wall has been blocked off but is clearly visible from the outside. Unfortunately, the transept's width merely emphasises what a short and stubby church this is. The awkwardness is offset somewhat by the distraction of a classical bullseye window set in the transept's south wall and carved in Cotswold limestone (and do have a good look at that overly elaborate finial above it – it's an attempt to hide the chimney for the fireplace within).

The transept is home to the church's two great treasures. A tympanum tells the tale of a kilted man running through a forest of acanthus shrubs to solicit the aid of a dove while being pursued by a dragon and a serpent. It probably once graced a doorway in the south wall (facing the village) which was lost when the transept was added. The carving is an outstanding example of the work of the Herefordshire School and would have been produced in about 1140.

Beneath it is a stone that, in all likelihood, first served as the base of a cross. It is carved on three sides, two of which bear Anglo-Saxon images: one of trees and the other a pattern of lozenges. The third side dates from the 12th century and shows Christ holding hands with a behaloed figure who is otherwise too mutilated to be identifiable. The image is usually interpreted as representing the Harrowing of Hell – when Christ made his triumphal visit to Hades in the period between his death and his resurrection.

Unusually, visitors are allowed up into the gallery. Another Whalley confection, it affords a grandstand view of the nave, the red sandstone sanctuary arch (Whalley again) and the Romanesque apse beyond. The staff of the manor would sit here during services, with the boxed seat at the north end reserved for the butler or steward.

Happily, this is one church that the Victorians more or less left alone, so virtually everything here today would be familiar to Bernard Whalley. Notable exceptions are the west porch and the octagonal font (both probably 18th century), the furniture in the eastern side of the nave (late 19th century), the

wooden triptych altarpiece (carved in 1907 by Mary, Marchioness of Hertford) and, of course, his own burial slab.

Back outside, the dead – mostly from the Badger family – lie among nettles. Squirrels scamper about in the limes and horse chestnuts, and sheep graze where the village once stood. Declared redundant in 1976, the church's fall from importance is all but complete. You can't help but feel that the church laments the passing of time and longs for the days when it was the focus of attention rather than an oddity hidden away among trees, overshadowed by a luxury hotel.

LANGLEY CHAPEL
RUCKLEY

Step over the threshold to feast your eyes on a unique example of what the inside of an early 17th-century Anglican church really looked like.

SPIRITUAL ORIENTATION
Church of England (English Heritage)

PHYSICAL ORIENTATION
Ruckley, Acton Burnell, Shropshire SY5 7HU
Grid reference: SJ 538 000
OS Landranger map 126

PUBLIC TRANSPORT
From Shrewsbury railway station (various train companies) take the 540 bus (boultonsofshropshire.com; 01694 771226) to Acton Burnell, from where it's a 1.25-mile walk to the chapel, first south almost to Ruckley and then left towards Langley Hall. The church is on the right.

OPENING ARRANGEMENTS
10am–6pm daily (late March to October)
10am–4pm daily (November to late March)
No admission is charged.

SERVICES
None.

on't let Langley Chapel's plain looks deceive you. Inside its trim but unremarkable façade is a 17th-century interior that the intervening years have left entirely unaltered, affording us an unparalleled glimpse into the well-ordered world of the post-Reformation Anglican church.

Marooned in a farmer's field, the fate of so many of the best churches, Langley Chapel is a simple nave-and-chancel rectangle built of grey sandstone. The roughly dressed blocks have weathered to different shades of grey or beige to form an indistinct patchwork that in a strange way renders the walls invisible. Of course, this is not because you can see through them but rather that there is so little about them to catch the eye that one's gaze is instantly diverted to any and every other point of interest in the building. This is tougher than one might suppose because there is a distinct dearth of the latter. The windows are plain and rationed to one per wall. The roof is of stone tiles, their stoicism in the face of four centuries of weather showing in every furrow, like the lines in the forehead of a nonagenarian who has seen too much. The unassuming weatherboarded bell-tower is by far the most striking exterior feature of the chapel.

The building goes back to 1313, when Richard Burnell, lord of the manor of Langley, received the necessary authority to construct himself a chapel. His work has

all but disappeared: the current church is largely a late Tudor affair. Later in the 14th century the estate came into the hands of the Lee family. Members of the clan refurbished the chapel around 1546 and again in the early 1600s. It is this second refurbishment that has been preserved as if in aspic. Less than a hundred years later the chapel was barely being used, though it struggled on until 1871 when its final regular service was held.

It is when you enter – using the more westerly of the two nail-studded Tudor doors in the south wall – that the magic is revealed. Langley Chapel is a glorious sea of furnishings of different types but all of the same mid-brown wood. It is, it must be said, a very calm sea, for everything is well ordered and in its right place. White walls, plain but for a frieze of roses and fleurs-de-lys, provide a perfect backdrop for showing off the furniture. Patterned medieval tiles in various shades of red cover the floor. The roof is a riot of geometric designs.

The church is described by its owners, English Heritage, as a 'unique survival of the way Anglican churches were arranged in the 17th century'. The word 'arranged' is particularly important, because so much of the Anglican way of worship at that time is explained not only by what you see in this church but by how it is set out.

The Reformation was the 16th-century movement that sought to address abuses of doctrine and practice within Roman Catholicism. Before its instigation, the altar was the centrepiece of the church. This was habitually made of stone, slightly elevated, and always at the far eastern (and thus holiest) extremity of the church. The high point of any service was the Mass, given at the altar in Latin, a language incomprehensible to all but the most learned, few of whom would be counted among the congregation.

Once the Reformation got into its stride, stone altars were removed from churches en masse. Mass became Communion and was led by the priest in English. Furthermore, this element of the service gave way to the primacy of the Word of God, as expressed in the reading of it and the sermonising upon it (often at interminable length). So at Langley we see a simple wooden table serving for an altar (sadly the original was stolen but it has been replaced with a copy). Unlike the altar, it is not set against the wall. This allowed Communion to be taken with the congregation grouped all around it, replicating the popular image of the Last Supper. The theological differences between Puritans and non-Puritans are also provided for. The former could simply sit on the benches during Communion while the latter could kneel (an act seen as 'popish' by the Puritans) at the kneeling desks placed in front of them.

The hexagonal pulpit is modest compared with the imposing creations often installed in churches (including several in this book) to emphasise the newly espoused prominence of preaching. However, this is more than made up for by the reading desk. As the name suggests, this was the place from which the Bible was read aloud during a service. This one is missing its lectern and sounding board but is large enough to accommodate seats. It also has a roof, which is very rare.

The seating arrangements reflect the social order of the day. The benches at the back of the church were for use by those on the lower rungs of society: individuals in service or manual labour. They looked at the backs of the heads of farmers and middle-ranking workers such as merchants who took their seats in small box pews. The chapel's sole spacious box pew was reserved for the lords of the manor, the Lee family. Naturally, this took pride of place right in front of the pulpit. Church musicians, more for reasons of practicality than social status, sat at the back at their own desk. This is another piece of ecclesiastical furniture seldom seen today.

Avid students of 17th-century Anglicanism will find in Langley Chapel a treasure trove. The rest of us will be happy to admire it for the wonderful time capsule that it is and for the composition of restrained elegance that it presents. ◈

30 ST MARY'S
SNIBSTON

See the Grumpy Jesus window in which a surly Messiah grudgingly blesses his flock.

SPIRITUAL ORIENTATION
Church of England

PHYSICAL ORIENTATION
St Mary's Lane, Snibston, Leicestershire LE67 3BN
Grid reference: SK 411 131
OS Landranger map 129

PUBLIC TRANSPORT
There is no public transport to Snibston but, from Loughborough railway station (eastmidlandstrains. co.uk; 03457 125678) you can walk to Fennel Street and catch the no. 16 bus to Memorial Square in Coalville. From there a no. 9A bus (both arrivabus.co.uk; 0344 8004411) will whisk you to The Plough in Ravenstone. It's a half-mile walk along Jenny's Lane and then St Mary's Lane to the church.

OPENING ARRANGEMENTS
Open in daylight hours 'as a place of quiet for prayer and reflection'.

SERVICES
8.30am 2nd Sunday (Holy Communion)
3.30pm (winter) 3rd Sunday (Evensong)
6pm (summer) 3rd Sunday (Evensong).

 nibston is one of those off-piste villages that you would only happen to go through if you were lost. The fact that it also finds itself in Leicestershire, a county that does not suffer from unsustainable levels of tourism, means that relatively few people will have seen its little church.

Enclosed by farmland on three sides and farm buildings on the fourth, St Mary's is a humble affair built of medieval rubble topped by a plain tiled roof. The gravestones on the slight slope to the south of the church are set in very tidy ranks like soldiers on parade. Many of the headstones are exactly alike and share a uniform style of inscription, as if this were a war cemetery.

The nave and chancel are a single unit, and where other churches might have a spire, a tower or at the very least a bell-cote, St Mary's has a plain and spindly wooden cross attached to the stone gable. It resembles the sort of cross used in high churches for processions and looks like it might have been put up on the roof by

some farm boys as a prank and left there because no one can find a tall enough ladder to get it down again. The church is porchless – the building's only projections being two buttresses on the south side that keep the fabric of the place together.

It's as well that they do really, because St Mary's has not always made a success of keeping itself in one piece. As a calligraphied notice inside explains, in J. Nichol's *History and Antiquities of Leicestershire* (c.1810), the church is recorded as possessing a small chancel as well as a tower with a spire on top. These last two became unsafe and were pulled down at some unknown date. In 1739, the parishioners used the material from the tower and spire to restore the west wall. They hung a brand-new bell the same year. Come 1804, the church required more attention, this time with the east wall being rebuilt. There was clearly some money splashing about at this time because, according to another handwritten notice, all five windows you see in the church today were installed that year (though, confusingly, Pevsner dates the four lancet windows to 1847).

At least the plain round-arched doorway in the south wall seems to have held its own over the years. It may be as old as 13th century, which may also have been when the church was built. The font might be of the same vintage, though the basin was rechiselled in the 1847 restoration. Look carefully though and, within the foliage design that runs around the middle of the basin, you'll make out a small snake and two faces. These are a reminder that the serpent caused Adam and Eve to turn away from God and that only baptism into Christ can provide a solution to the problem of original sin.

The altar table is the next most venerable item in the church and apparently dates from the time of the Civil War. On either side of it are two boards bearing the Ten Commandments, the Apostles' Creed and the Lord's Prayer. Between them stands a rather extraordinary round-headed window depicting a remarkably grumpy Jesus. Sullen of face, he is making sure everyone can see the keyhole-like stigmata in his hands, though he does not quite manage to thrust a foot far enough forward from his cloak to show us the hole in that as well. Quite what effect the artist was attempting to achieve can only be guessed at.

The window was given in 1878 by Elizabeth and Sarah Hextall 'to the glory of God and in memory of all their relations here asleep'. The two sisters sleep here themselves now. They died in the 1880s having both reached their 80s, fine adverts for the benefits of spinsterhood. If you venture down to the corner of the churchyard where the two yew trees stand you'll see their graves at one end of the

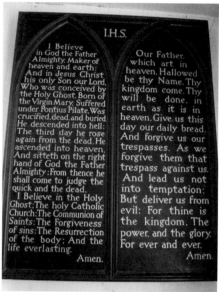

ranks of headstones amidst the Hextalls they remembered.

The tetchy Jesus is offset by another window in which a sad and tender Saviour holds a lamb while a ewe and a ram – possibly the parents – nuzzle his legs. In this depiction, Jesus has managed to poke both his feet out so the stigmata are showing.

Notwithstanding the fact that this window might just be Edwardian, any Victorian returning here today would feel rather at home for there is little that they would not recognise beyond the electric lights, heaters and fancy modern keyboard (though even that is next to a comfortingly venerable harmonium). They would also be appreciative of the fact that St Mary's is clearly not a church that tries to show off. It seems quite content as an obscure church serving an obscure hamlet, and there's a great deal of charm in that.

Finally, do not be alarmed if, on entering the church, you experience a mysterious ringing in your ear. As a notice in the church rather winsomely advises: 'The small tinkling bell is somewhere in the roof above the ceiling.'

When the churchwardens find a long enough ladder to get that cross down from outside, they'll no doubt have a look in the loft to see if they can possibly locate the mischievous little thing.

MILLDALE CHAPEL

MILLDALE

The modesty of this little place of worship reflects the down-to-earth nature of the congregations who have worshipped here.

SPIRITUAL ORIENTATION

Methodist

PHYSICAL ORIENTATION

Millway Lane, Milldale, Alstonefield, Derbyshire DE6 2GB
Grid reference: SK 139 547
OS Landranger map 119

PUBLIC TRANSPORT

From Buxton railway station (northernrail.org) walk the short distance to Terrace Road and take the MC3 bus (derbyshirect.co.uk; 01335 300670) to Millway Lane in Milldale. The church is on the right as you come out of Milldale, just after Dove Chapel Cottage.

OPENING ARRANGEMENTS

Always open.

SERVICES

2pm Easter Saturday
7pm 1st Wednesday (June, July and August)
4pm Christmas Eve
For further details ring 01335 324404.

nlike the vast majority of churches in this book, it is possible to walk past Milldale Chapel without realising it's there. If there were awards given for the most unassuming church in Britain, this one would have to have an acceptance speech prepared pretty much permanently. A simple white-painted building, its gable facing a steep road that climbs out of the village, Milldale Chapel might very easily be mistaken for a small house. Indeed, if it weren't for the two plaques on the wall either side of the door that give away its identity, the locals would be forever having to point it out to visitors. There is no churchyard, and the grounds consist of a few square feet of grass at the front

divided by a two-stride path from the road to the front door.

There was a Primitive Methodist 'society' in this fold of the Peak District from about 1810. The grass-roots working-class movement had begun three years earlier in the Potteries and the Milldale society's establishment was the work of John Benton and Eleazor Hathorn, into whose missionary patch Dovedale fell. Eleazor was a colourful figure – his loss of a leg fighting Napoleon I cannot have made his journeys up hill and down dale easy.

However, it wasn't until January 1836 that the dissenters of Milldale had their own chapel. It was built of stone on a granite rock, and hard work it must have been bringing it to completion at that time

of year. It formed part of the Methodist Church's Leek Circuit but, in 1906, William Radnor reported in an article in the *Christian Messenger* that the chapel had been 'gladly given over... a few years since' to the Ashbourne Circuit. One wonders what tales lay behind that 'gladly'. He added a cautionary note:

The scenery here is magnificently grand – the lofty mountains, deep valleys, and winding rivers will well repay a visit, but I advise our readers not to go in winter, unless they belong to the sturdy enduring type of which Derbyshire local preachers are made.

Fans of towering reredos or ornately carved doorways will be disappointed here. Milldale is not a fancy place nor has ever sought to be so. The whole ethos of the Primitive Methodists – indeed, the reason why they were known by that epithet – was to return to the simpler, purer form of Methodism propounded by its founder John Wesley. This in turn had taken its inspiration from the early Christian church. The movement campaigned for social justice and many of its members went on to become Chartists, trade union leaders and, in later years, members of the Labour Party. Its adherents were also keen to liberate themselves from what they saw as the fripperies of religious worship and the ostentatiousness of the church buildings used by other denominations.

It should come as no surprise, therefore, that the chapel has more the feel of a living room than a church. The windows are rectangular and plain and domestic. A solid little harmonium sits in the corner, trying not to draw attention to itself. The pulpit, if it can be described by that name, is low and unobtrusive, its only decoration a brace of crosses. Behind the altar table, hung on dark wooden panelling, is a small framed watercolour of the dove of peace by artist Wendy Peat – an apt symbol for a chapel that guards the northern end of Dovedale. The only elements that could be described as even faintly high church are the candle-holders on the walls around the chapel, including two that, in a fancier church, might have been connected by an altar rail. Some might denigrate the overall effect as dull and uninspiring: the Primitive Methodists would doubtless call it unaffected, earthy and free of distractions.

Sadly, the congregation dwindled to a point where weekly Sunday services became untenable and the last regular meetings were held in 1986. However, rather than close the church, the decision was taken to keep it open as a place where the two million walkers and other tourists who pass through Dovedale each year could find a little tranquillity and, perhaps, spiritual nourishment.

Thus visitors will encounter here a pile of small stones inscribed with a Bible verse and a cross sitting below a sign inviting them to take one 'to remember your visit to this place'. The chapel is also one of 13 churches on the Peak Pilgrimage (peakpilgrimage.org.uk), a 34-mile route from Ilam (once home to Saxon hermit St Bertram) to Eyam, the heroic community that sealed itself off from the world in order not to spread the plague, an action that cost 260 of the villagers their lives.

The welcoming attitude found at Milldale Chapel is heart-warming. Those who look after the little place are thrilled for visitors to come in, even if only to get out of the rain or catch a few moments of respite from the outside world.

STEETLEY CHAPEL

STEETLEY

The 14th-century tombstone of the quietly heroic Lawrence le Leche is most affecting.

SPIRITUAL ORIENTATION

Church of England

PHYSICAL ORIENTATION

Dumb Hall Lane, Steetley, near Whitwell, Derbyshire S80 3DZ
Grid reference: SK 543 787
OS Landranger map 120

PUBLIC TRANSPORT

The chapel is about 2 miles from Whitwell railway station and 3 miles from Worksop station (both eastmidlandstrains.co.uk; 03457 125678). The 77 bus (stagecoachbus.com; 01246 211007) travels between the two towns and will get you to the junction with the Chesterfield Road (A619), 1.5 miles from the chapel, though the subsequent walk along this busy road is not recommended. Steetley Lane heads north off the A619 and the chapel is located at the Dumb Hall Lane turning.

OPENING ARRANGEMENTS

10am–4pm daily.

SERVICES

3.15pm 2nd Sunday (Said Eucharist)
In July, the service is held outside the church.

here's so much to enjoy at this church that it's difficult to know where to begin. If you're not won over by this immoderately handsome building at very first glance (and most people are), then there's the hugely impressive doorway, the riotous stained-glass window and the poignant story of Lawrence le Leche to enjoy, along with the brilliant trick played by the chapel's Norman designer of making anyone who enters his small church feel as if they're in a cathedral.

Also known as All Saints' Church, the chapel was built in the middle of the 12th century. Ironically, for a structure that has been feted as one of the most exquisite examples of a Norman church the country has to offer, it was actually crafted by homegrown Saxons. It was, however, probably commissioned by a man with roots across the Channel. The prevailing theory is that he was a nobleman called Gley Le Breton and that he had it built as his private chapel during the reign of King Stephen (1135–54). He handed it down to his daughter Matilda and it passed from one important family to another over the centuries. However, it eventually fell into disrepair and spent most of the 19th century roofless and used by pigs and sheep, only to be given a radical restoration in 1880 by one J L Pearson, the Surveyor of Westminster Abbey.

It's inevitable that a church that was around in the time of King John and is situated close to Sherwood Forest should find itself tangled up in the legend of Robin Hood. Friar Tuck is credited with coercing Robin and his Merry Men into coming here to say their prayers. Alan-a-Dale is said to have been wedded here (a claim disputed by St James's church in Papplewick), while a false ceiling reputedly provided Robin with a hiding place up in the rafters. To cap it all, the master outlaw is said to lie sleeping in the soil of the neighbouring farm.

Admirably less mythical is the story of Lawrence le Leche, whose tombstone was found lying across the doorway to the chapel, and which now stands in the nave.

The stone does not bear his name but instead is engraved with several crosses, a three-legged altar holding a chalice and plate (for giving Communion), and a hand

might be his, was discovered by the tombstone. On his deathbed he had asked that he be buried in the entranceway so that the faithful might step on him on their way to their devotions.

The chapel they entered is built of smooth, expertly shaped stones and has the clean-cut appearance of a mathematical diagram. Its apse is a semicircle, its chancel a square and its nave a rectangle – one almost expects to be asked to calculate the area of the floor. All such thoughts are cast aside though when confronted with the entrance portal. Although much of it is Pearson's reconstruction of eroded Norman work, it is a thing of great majesty. Five arches are supported by pillars and crowned with a triangular facing. The carvings on the pillars repay closer inspection: see if you can make out a mermaid (or siren), two fish, a pelican and the Good Shepherd saving a lamb from a bear.

Step through the door and immediately the narrowness of the nave, the stick-thin lancet windows and the exaggerated height of a roof lost in an upper darkness combine to give the illusion of a cathedral.

Take a moment to look up at the capitals of the pillars on the north side of the Romanesque chancel arch. You'll find a lion with two bodies and St George delivering a dutifully distressed damsel from the depraved designs of a dragon.

that comes out to bless the viewer. The man these devices commemorate was appointed to Steetley Chapel in 1348, the year before the arrival of one of the many terrible plagues that cut a swathe through medieval Britain. It accounted for 77 priests in Derbyshire alone, with a further 22 fleeing their posts. Lawrence chose to stay to offer solace to the dying and to give what medical help he could. Le Leche is a name that marks him out as a healer – it's derived from the leeches that doctors would apply to patients to drain 'bad' blood. He served those around him for seven years until, inevitably, he himself succumbed to the plague. A skull, which

Pass under the arch to the chancel and you can't help but see the one feature that is later than the Norman period. It is the only large window in the chapel and was installed in 1990. Depicting Christ as the Risen Lamb of God, it's a bold and striking affair, its blood-red summit giving way to softer blues and greens as it descends to earth, with the chancel and a few local buildings featured at the bottom.

The apse contains another representation of the Lamb of God, though this one has not yet risen from death. It can be found in the medallion where the stone ribs of the vaulted roof meet, directly above the altar.

Here again, the capitals of two of the pillars are worthy of attention: one shows Adam, Eve, the serpent and the tree of knowledge; while another bears two doves. Taken together they represent a text from the Gospel of Matthew: 'Be ye therefore wise as serpents, and harmless as doves.' The space is lit by three small lancets filled with 1920s glass whose simple abstract designs are every bit as mesmerising as the substantial chancel window.

In case all this general gloriousness has managed to transport you somewhere up in the clouds, just before you leave the chapel you will be brought back down to Derbyshire with a bump. A small notice at the exit reads: 'Please make sure this door is snecked.' 🕮

167

ST MARY'S
LEAD

The five grave slabs set into the floor of the nave are crammed with heraldic inscriptions to decipher.

SPIRITUAL ORIENTATION

Private chapel (Churches Conservation Trust)

PHYSICAL ORIENTATION

Lead, Saxton, Tadcaster, Yorkshire LS24 9QN
Grid reference: SE 464 368
OS Landranger map 105

PUBLIC TRANSPORT

From Church Fenton railway station (northernrail.org) take the 492 bus (arrivabus.co.uk; 0344 8004411) to the little village of Saxton, from where it's a mile to St Mary's, the last portion of which is a footpath across a field opposite The Crooked Billet pub.

OPENING ARRANGEMENTS

Open daily.

SERVICES

An annual service is held on a Sunday afternoon each May and there's a carol singing event in December. Check leadchurch.org.uk and the 'St Mary's Church, Lead' Facebook page for details.

oor old St Mary's. She cuts a rather Eeyore-like figure, a tiny thing sitting all alone in a boggy field, exposed to the worst the Yorkshire climate can throw at her. It wasn't ever thus. Once upon a time this private chapel to a manor house was an opulent place twice its current size, even running to a gilded ceiling. It was not alone either but part of a medieval settlement whose protuberances can be made out in the same field.

Though 14th century in origin, it is destined to be forever associated with an event that occurred on Palm Sunday 1461: the Battle of Towton. The Cock Beck, the insignificant stream visitors must step across to reach the church, marked the western extent of this battle of the War of the Roses and, as is often the way with streams on battlefields, it is said to have run red with the blood of the fallen. In this case, however, there may be some justification for believing that it did just that, for Towton is thought to be the bloodiest battle ever fought on English soil, with 10,000 dead (some chroniclers put the figure at 28,000) and double that number wounded. The engagement tore Henry VI of Lancaster from the throne, handing the crown to Edward, Duke of York. St Mary's is the only building on or around the site of the battlefield that remains standing.

However, it may not be the oldest church on that site. A 9th- or 10th-century 'hog back' grave-slab discovered here points to the existence of an earlier construction, possibly of timber. The current church used to be about double the size it is now, with a large chancel at the east end. It is not known when this was lost, though it's helpfully marked out so that visitors are able to visualise where it was and what the church would have looked like.

The building the 21st century inherited is a plain rectangle with a stone bell-cote (the bell went missing sometime in the last century). Its windows are in the Decorated style (sometimes known as Decorated Gothic), as was fashionable in the 14th century. There's no churchyard, this being merely a chapelry with no priest of its own and no burial rights, though some interments did occur within the church itself.

The first surprise comes when you turn to close the door and find that it has had important events in the life of the church scribbled all over it. The graffiti date back to the 1784 restoration, when

the door was probably also hung. The rather wonderful pulpit parked up in a corner at the opposite end is likely to have been installed at the same time. It has three distinct parts: a clerk's pew, a pew from which to read the Bible, and a pulpit. The congregational pews, simple but agreeable affairs, may be a little older, perhaps late medieval. Even earlier is the font, which is Norman.

Once your eyes have adjusted to the dark – even on a sunny day it's far from bright inside – you'll be able to make out some wooden boards on the walls which have what appear at first glance to be somewhat arcane texts on them (the three written in capital letters are quotations from a service of Holy Communion). Look closely at the sign that begins, 'This is His commandment…' and you'll notice it's a palimpsest. Whoever painted it was not able to obliterate the original wording, leaving the phrase 'AND NEEDY THE LORD' clearly visible.

But it's the floor that holds the church's greatest treasures. Some of the huge grave-slabs, strewn with heraldic symbols, are actually older than the building itself and give you a sense of having been transported back into a time of knights and chivalrous deeds. Most of the ledger stones commemorate members of the Tyas family who were probably responsible for the construction of the church. One of them reads, in Norman French, *Priez Pvr Lalme Franconis Tiesci Ici Gist Chevalier,* which translates into English as 'Pray for the soul of Franco Tyas, Knight, who lies here'. Another slab shows a chalice, indicating that the corpse beneath once belonged to a priest.

Over the centuries the church's fortunes have waxed and waned – in 1596 it was observed to be 'in utter Ruyne and decay' and such a state prevailed again at the beginning of the last century.

Fortunately, in 1931 a group of walkers led by Jack Winterburn, David Sayle and W Aitken took the church under its wing and brought it back from the brink. Aside from the general repairs they made (as recorded on the church door), they also installed the stone altar and placed the medieval slab on top. Ever since, St Mary's has been known as the Ramblers' Church. It was re-dedicated the following year but, with the local population dwindling, was declared redundant in 1980. On this occasion the Churches Conservation Trust stepped into the breach.

Despite the fact that much of the furniture in the church dates from long after the War of the Roses, in the penumbral light, with the smell of damp filling the air, it doesn't take much to imagine the Battle of Towton raging just outside. Just be thankful it isn't. 🍂

ST ETHELBURGA'S
GREAT GIVENDALE

The late-Norman chancel arch, complete with bas-relief Green Man faces, is a thing of great joy.

SPIRITUAL ORIENTATION
Church of England

PHYSICAL ORIENTATION
Beacon Road, Great Givendale, Pocklington, Yorkshire YO42 1TT
Grid reference: SE 813 538
OS Landranger map 106

PUBLIC TRANSPORT
Travel to York railway station (virgintrainseastcoast.com; crosscountrytrains.co.uk; grandcentralrail.com; tpexpress.co.uk) where you can pick up a no. 747 bus (eyms.co.uk; 01482 592929) that passes near Great Givendale on its way to Bishop Wilton (1.75 miles) and you might find a friendly bus driver who will drop you off at the end of Givendale Lane (0.5 miles).

OPENING ARRANGEMENTS
Always open.

SERVICES
9.15am 2nd Sunday (Matins)
9.15am 4th Sunday (Holy Communion)
All services are candlelit.
Further details at pocklingtongroupofchurches.org.

od bless the Misses Singleton. If it were not for their efforts, St Ethelburga's wonderful chancel arch would no longer be with us. In the Romanesque style, with a zigzag pattern, it was created in 1150 and sports some thrillingly woebegone bas-relief Green Man faces with cords running in and out of their mouths or noses. If only they could look out of the window they would surely cheer up a bit, for St Ethelburga's is cradled by trees and set on a little ledge of level ground overlooking a deep bowl of land, at the bottom of which is a large pond fringed with trees. In spring, when the aconites and snowdrops creep out of the woods to carpet the churchyard, it makes for a charming scene indeed.

The 12th-century church that stood on this spot was totally rebuilt in 1849, largely at the expense of the second of four local John Singletons, each one of whom begat the next. The family produced three jockeys and won the renowned flat race the St Leger twice. John Singleton I rode for the future prime minister, the Marquess of Rockingham, and was generally reckoned 'the best jockey in England' in his day. He was clearly very successful because the money he earned from his profession allowed him to buy Manor Farm (now known as Manor House and

Manor Cottage), which became the family seat. His son John enjoyed a lucrative career as a land agent, enlarging the estate to 700 acres. He was 79 and just a few years from the end of his life when he and the local ratepayers footed the bill to have St Ethelburga's restored. It is not known which of the 12 daughters of the third John Singleton were responsible for saving the chancel arch – the act is merely accredited to the 'Misses Singletons' – but nine of those alive in 1849 were single at the time, so you can take your pick from Ann, Jane, Maria, Rebecca, Elizabeth, Susannah, Theresa, Lucy and Julia.

As can be seen at a glance from the gate at the top of the path that leads down to the entrance, the church was more or less razed to the ground and built all over again, largely copying its 13th-century

stylings. Most of the stone of the original church suffered the ignominy of being carted off to mend local roads but the distaff side of the Singleton family intervened to ensure that at least some of the church's treasures were saved this fate. Thus, along with the Norman chancel arch, there are two 13th-century windows; a stoup from the same era; and a small brass plaque from 1641 that now adorns the north wall of the chancel. This last, written in Latin, gives a lesson in what was thought important in a man and a woman in Stuart times. While the husband, George Jackson, is described as 'true, open, with gentle wisdom, the finest of fathers, strong, loyal to his country and worthy', his wife Barbera (sic) Allan is valued only by her appearance, her conformity to sexual mores and her ability to produce babies (she is 'beautiful, chaste and blessed by many children'). It could be argued that societal attitudes have changed precious little since.

Another plaque, commemorating Jonathan Atkins, has a far darker side. Atkins was a sometime governor of Barbados and is rumoured to have bragged to Charles II that 'in the Caribbean one black man can do the work of three white

men' – a notion that helped spark Britain's involvement in the slave trade.

Unusually, there are windows in only one side of the nave. Presumably it was felt unnecessary to put windows into the north side where a stand of trees blocks any view. Most of the action takes place in the south wall of the chancel: aside from a medieval window, there is a sedile, and a piscina with a trefoil head next to it. Meanwhile, at the back of the church, the simple stone font is overwhelmed by an elaborately carved wooden cover that stretches almost up to the ceiling and is lifted off by means of a pulley.

St Ethelburga, to whom the church is dedicated, is strangely absent, the only stained-glass window featuring Christ and 11 angels. It's fair to say her life was beset by a multitude of fellow saints. Both her parents, Aethelbert and Bertha, and her brother, Erconwald, were canonised, as was Enflaeda, the only child of hers not to die young or in infancy. Her husband, King Edwin of Northumbria, also achieved sainthood, though only after she converted him. When he was killed fighting the heathen King of Mercia in 632, Queen Ethelburga escaped by sea to the court of her brother, King Edbald. He handed her the remains of a Roman villa at Lyming in Kent and it was there that she founded a nunnery, the first ever in England.

The rebuilding in 1849 of her little outpost in the Yorkshire Wolds coincided with the death of the artist William Etty, a great friend of the Singletons who spent time with them in Great Givendale. His paintings of the church are now in the possession of the York Art Gallery. Closer at hand – in a folder at the back of the church – are some (sadly non-Etty) prints of sketches of St Ethelburga's that can be yours in exchange for a donation. 🎴

ST LEONARD'S
SPEETON

Look for the simple but rather affecting 12th-century Agnus Dei discovered in 1965.

SPIRITUAL ORIENTATION
Church of England

PHYSICAL ORIENTATION
Off Main Street, Speeton, Yorkshire YO14 9TD
Grid reference: TA 151 747
OS Landranger map 101

PUBLIC TRANSPORT
From Bridlington railway station (northernrail.org) take the short walk to the bus station where you can board the 121 bus (eyms. co.uk; 01482 592929) to Speeton Lane End. It's less than half a mile from there to the church.

OPENING ARRANGEMENTS
Open during daylight hours.

SERVICES
11am 1st Sunday (Holy Communion)
11am 2nd & 3rd Sunday (Service of the Word)
11am 4th Sunday (Matins)
See headlandbenefice.co.uk for details.

he board outside St Leonard's proudly proclaims it to be 'One of the oldest and smallest churches in Yorkshire. Built by the Saxons, used by the Danes, restored by the Normans.' They might have continued, 'Enjoyed by the Elizabethans,' because many a modern-day pilgrim's feet propel them here. Then again, the signwriter might also have added 'Not particularly enjoyed by Charlotte Brontë,' so perhaps it's as well they stopped when they did.

This early Norman church – one of the smallest parish churches in the whole of Yorkshire – comprises a nave, chancel and tower, all of cut stone and a small quantity of chalk. Though it was built around 1100 or earlier, an even more ancient church probably stood on this same site, as is often the way with Norman churches. It began life under the aegis of the Augustinian Priory at Bridlington and not a great deal of note appears to have happened to it until Henry VIII dissolved the priory.

The Reformation saw St Leonard's stripped of its 'popery' – losing, among other things, its stone altar, a fresco of the Crucifixion and a statue of St Leonard. Although the 18th century saw it newly furnished with a three-decker pulpit and box pews, by 1831 it had hit the skids. The

chancel end was being used as a school and a topographer named Rev Prickett summed up St Leonard's plight in seven words: 'Speeton Chapel is only an oblong room.' It was faring no better 21 years later when Charlotte Brontë came calling and reported:

> *It was certainly not more than thrice the length of our passage, floored with brick, the walls green with mould, the pews painted white, but the paint almost worn off with time and decay.*

Today St Leonard's enjoys much ruder health – step through the door and there's an immediate sense that this is very much a church in use rather than a museum piece. The clock set to show the day's high tide is also a reminder of where we are – just a field or two from clifftops that look out over the North Sea.

This proximity to the coast, along with its relative remoteness, led to the tale that it was used by smugglers. During the 17th and 18th centuries, services here were few and far between (in 1743 there was one held only every six weeks), which would certainly have made it a handy warehouse for illicit goods, but whether there is any truth to the story it's impossible to say.

A low and narrow arch separates the chancel from the nave. This latter space is

filled with attractive dark oak pews that came from the former Hostel of the Resurrection in Leeds (provider of accommodation to impoverished trainees for the ministry) and replaced early 20th-century pine pews which had themselves supplanted the box pews.

The pine pews had been brought in as part of a restoration project led by the Rev John Wilkinson, Vicar of Bempton and Speeton, around 1911. He also exchanged the pulpit for a new one, removed the plaster ceiling (chunks of which were known to drop onto individuals worshipping below – occasions which it would be hard not to take as some sort of message from God), and installed a new organ. The brick floor was pulled up, tiles laid down and a brace of lancet windows put into the west wall flanking the tower. His pulpit has since been swapped for the lectern that graces the church today.

Elements of St Leonard's that largely escaped all this upheaval are the plain circular Saxon font that bears the scars of its extreme old age; some niches, including one with a canopy in the east wall that may have been home to a statuette of St Leonard before it was swept away in the tidal wave of the Reformation;

and a stone box into which pilgrims could place some token of their devotion.

A stone bearing the image of a circular cross was unearthed during restoration work in 1910. This may well have been a consecration cross marking a spot anointed by the bishop in order to sanctify the church for Christian worship. Set in the north wall, it has been joined by a small modern figurine of the crucified Christ. However, it was the restoration undertaken in 1965 that uncovered the church's great treasure. Above the south door a stone was found bearing the Agnus Dei (Lamb of God) in bas-relief. It shows a lamb carrying a cross – expertly balancing it in the crook of one of its front legs – and was carved in the 1120s. Though probably unintentional, the lamb appears to be smiling.

Lastly, there's an interesting exhibition of photos including some of the church in former times. Also featured are some shipwrecked vessels that can still be seen on the shore below and soldiers billeted at nearby Church Farm immediately after the evacuation from Dunkirk in 1940.

Outside, the tower tapers slightly as it heads upwards. It supports a ship's bell in a bell-cote topped with a comically small finial. It's as if the architect made a disastrous error with regard to scale when transmitting his plans to the builder à la Spinal Tap's Nigel Tufnel. Meanwhile, if you look very closely on the south wall you may make out the remains of a mass clock (see Old Church of St Mary the Virgin, p52, and St Hubert's, p58).

The dearth of a churchyard obliged pall-bearers to stagger all the way over to Bridlington Priory, nearly 5 miles away. The so-called 'corpse road' was once quite obvious but has since disappeared. A rather less sombre journey can be made after your visit by walking the short path from the church to the cliffs, where there's a magnificent view along the coast. 🦌

ST LEONARD'S
CHAPEL-LE-DALE

Look out for the anchor-and-cross gravestone of Tom and Isobella Kilburn.

SPIRITUAL ORIENTATION
Church of England

PHYSICAL ORIENTATION
Oddie's Lane, Chapel-le-Dale, North Yorkshire LA6 3AR
Grid reference: SD 737 771
OS Landranger map 98

PUBLIC TRANSPORT
From Ribblehead railway station (northernrail.org) it's just over a 2-mile walk to Chapel-le-Dale along the straight but undulating Low Sleights Road.

OPENING ARRANGEMENTS
Open daily.

SERVICES
2.30pm 1st & 3rd Sunday (Evening Prayer)
2.30pm 2nd & 4th Sunday (Holy Communion)
NB In severe weather services may be cancelled at short notice.

ucked away behind trees, with pastureland around it, St Leonard's looks for all the world like a typical country church, albeit in miniature form. It's hard to imagine that just a skip and a hop away is the B6255, a high road that snakes its way for 17 miles between the fells from Ingleton to Hawes, mixing fantastic views of the immense hulk that is Ingleborough mountain with exposure to some of England's wettest and grimmest weather.

Built in the 16th century at the junction of an ancient trackway and a Roman road, St Leonard's probably started life as a chapel of ease attached to the parish church at Low Bentham. If that's the case, it would certainly have been a boon to local farming families, saving them an arduous 18-mile return journey

to church of a Sunday, a particularly unappealing prospect in the depths of winter. This explains why the church, constructed of local limestone, is a mere 48ft by 20ft. It might also account for its low roof, though a desire to keep the building hunkered down and out of the wind might also have been at play there. A simple rectangle with a porch, vestry and a shy little bell-cote, the beauty of the church lies in its unassuming character, skilfully brought out in a sketch by J M W Turner on his visit in 1808. Now held by the Tate, the rather faint drawing shows St Leonard's with Chapel Beck running below and Whernside mountain in the distance.

The most unusual feature of the church is that it's never actually been dedicated to the saint after which it is named. The fact that it is named after

St Leonard – the patron saint of prisoners and pregnant women – is down to an error made by a local historian in the 1940s. The first known reference to the church was in 1595 when it appears on the scene as 'the chaple of Wiersdall'. Just 23 years later it had become 'the chapelry of Witfalls'. By 1677, marriages at the church were recorded as being solemnised in 'chappell ith dale'. By the 18th century this had morphed again into the 'Chapel of Ingleton Fells' (Ingleton being just a couple of miles away) or simply the 'Fells Chapel'. In 1830, 'Chapel-le-Dale' makes its first appearance and this name, with or without the hyphens (an ambiguity that continues today), stuck until about 1940. It was then that one J L Hamer found a 1554 will

made by Richard Gibson that referred to 'the church of Saynte Leonard at Ingleton'. Since the church at Ingleton is St Mary's, Hamer decided that the church in question must be the one at Chapel-le-Dale. He convinced the vicar who promptly 'restored' the name to the church without dedicating it officially to St Leonard, since he assumed that that must already have been done in antiquity.

Unfortunately, a later historian, John Bentley, discovered a slew of other wills from the second half of the 16th century in which so many deceased Ingletonians referred to St Leonard's that it was evident that St Mary's must once have been known by that name. In all likelihood, the Chapel-le-Dale church was never dedicated to any saint. Still, St Leonard himself is probably quite happy to have attached his name to one of the two churches, having evidently been eased out in Ingleton.

The church underwent a thorough restoration in 1869. These are words that are capable of dousing the fires of even the most ardent church visitor. To be fair, however, the interior of St Leonard's has a warm domestic feel to it rather than the starched formality that the Victorians all too often visited upon churches. The stained-glass windows are a bit hit and miss though. One in which a less-pious-than-usual Jesus sits down to have a chat with the Samaritan woman at the well is refreshingly human. Another window depicts the risen Christ at Emmaus with two disciples who appear to be engaged in a jazz-hands dance routine.

More pleasing to the eye is the compact 19-pipe Lieblich organ tucked away at the back of the nave. However, it's a marble memorial on the west wall that is St Leonard's most affecting feature. The comma-heavy inscription reads:

> *To the memory of those, who*
> *through accidents lost their lives,*
> *in constructing the railway works,*
> *between Settle, and Dent Head.*
> *This tablet was erected at the joint*
> *expense, of their fellow workmen*
> *and the Midland Railway Company*
> *1869 to 1876.*

Around 1870 work started on both the 440yd Ribblehead Viaduct and the 1.5-mile Blea Moor Tunnel, both essential to the completion of the Settle to Carlisle railway line – now feted as one of the most scenic in Britain. Shockingly, around 215 lives were lost. While many died in worksite accidents, over half the fatalities were of babies and infants carried off by diseases such as smallpox contracted in the nearby shanty towns the navvies inhabited with their dependants. The dead soon filled up the churchyard at Chapel-le-Dale and new land had to be donated in order to accommodate the incessant flow of often heartbreakingly tiny coffins. The degree of poverty among this ill-starred group can be gauged by the fact that not one of the graves has a headstone.

By contrast, the churchyard's most arresting gravestone, hard by the church door, belongs to the year 1928 and to Tom and Isabella Kilburn of Hill Inn, who met their deaths on 11 January. From the anchor and chain draped around the cross that marks their grave it might be thought that they perished in a shipwreck. However, the anchor was simply a symbol of hope to Christians in the first few centuries AD.

Ironically, the link has best been maintained in the public consciousness by that purveyor of the demon drink, the public house, many of which in Britain are called The Hope and Anchor.

37 NORMAN CHAPEL
DURHAM CASTLE

The atmosphere of this ancient place makes simply being there a moving experience.

SPIRITUAL ORIENTATION

Church of England

PHYSICAL ORIENTATION

Durham Castle, 7 Owengate, Durham, Co. Durham DH1 3HB
Grid reference: NZ 273 423
OS Landranger map 88

PUBLIC TRANSPORT

From Durham railway station (virgintrainseastcoast.com; 03457 225111) it's less than a mile's walk down to the River Wear, across the Silver Street bridge and up the hill to the castle.

OPENING ARRANGEMENTS

Tickets for a guided tour of the castle (dur.ac.uk/durham.castle; 0191 3342932) must be purchased to enter the chapel. When there are no private events taking place, tours are normally conducted daily at 1.15pm, 2.15pm, 3.15pm and 4.15pm. Outside term time, there are usually also tours commencing at 10.15am, 11.15am and 12.15pm.

SERVICES

9pm Sunday (candlelit Compline) – sadly, this is only open to the students and faculty of Durham University.

ne of the most breathtaking places of worship of any size, the Norman Chapel inside Durham Castle has a feel of a tiny stone grove, at once an intimate and yet awe-inspiring space.

Though the castle was begun in 1072, the date of the chapel in its inner bailey is disputed. The accepted history has been that the Bishop of Durham, William Walcher, had it constructed in 1075. However, some academics have begun to argue quite compellingly that it was actually the brainchild of William de St Calais, the successor to Walcher after the latter was murdered by a band of disgruntled Northumbrians. William de St Calais was very close to his namesake, the Conqueror, and also seems to have been a key organiser of the Domesday Book. He was made bishop in 1080 and is likely to have started work on the chapel shortly afterwards (a sort of practice run for the nearby cathedral he would later design).

Whichever theory is correct, the chapel is one of the oldest parts of the castle to have survived to the present day. Immediately upon entering it you get a sense of having penetrated some long-lost

Egyptian tomb. In many ways it's an English variant on a vault deep in the bowels of a pyramid, for it has spent the vast majority of its life in silent darkness in the innards of the castle. More or less abandoned just 50 years after it was built, it became all but enveloped by other buildings and then made completely inaccessible when the keep mound was extended in the 14th or 15th century.

No one is thought to have set foot inside the tiny chapel again until the late 18th century. Even then there was no great appreciation of what the explorers had found – no Howard Carter exclaiming excitedly about the wonderful things he could see – and so it was left in peace once more.

In 1837, the castle became a university (no current seat of learning in the world occupies an older building). Three years later, needing a convenient access point to the keep – which had been rebuilt and made into student accommodation – the university authorities knocked two holes in the east and west walls of the chapel, turning it into a corridor.

It took a global conflict to end this indignity. In World War II the space was pressed into service as an RAF observation and command post. The lighting in the room was improved for the operators working there, who were thus also able to make out the carvings on the capitals of the pillars. At last it began to dawn on people what this room actually was. It seems unbelievable, therefore, that the chamber was used as the university bike shed into the early 1950s. Eventually, however, the hole that had been made in the east wall was filled in and the chapel reconsecrated.

The original doorway, at the west end of the south wall, has been blocked for centuries, so today access to the chapel is through a lobby and along a wide tunnel to the 19th-century western opening. Inside, the space is divided up by a little crop of pillars, their honeyed stone rippled with bands of iron. Look up at the capitals at the top of these and you'll see an array of excellently preserved carvings, probably crafted by William de St Calais' own Norman masons. They include numerous faces, naked men, star and foliage patterns (references, respectively, to heaven and paradise), a mermaid (representing temptation), and various lions. There is also a hunting scene thought to depict St Eustace, a man who was converted when he had a vision of a dazzlingly bright cross between the antlers of an enormous stag (see also St Hubert's, p58).

The walls are bare now but originally would have been plastered over and painted, probably in blocks of different colours. The north wall, through which the chapel receives its only (rather meagre) daylight, is also the curtain wall of the castle. The large opening visible here is a blocked sally port.

Deliciously, the chapel represents the final hurrah of a Saxon culture that was being brutally suppressed elsewhere. It's likely that Saxon masons were forced to work here and they have left to posterity their trademark deep-groin vaulting in the ceiling and the herringbone pattern of the floor tiles.

The chapel's years of entombment followed by ignorant misuse have actually been a blessing in disguise for it has come to us – at least as far as the interior is concerned – in very much the same form as it was when whichever Bishop William came here to kneel in prayer. Aside from the affronts visited upon the chapel by the university authorities in Victorian times (which were almost all reversed in the 1950s) and the blocking of the windows by sundry buildings, it has suffered no renovations to keep it from falling down or to make it conform to the ecclesiastical or architectural fashions of the day. Instead, this chapel brought into being by both Norman and Saxon hands has been passed down virtually unblemished from century to century. It is our great fortune that we live at a time in which the music finally stopped and the parcel was unwrapped for us to enjoy.

ST CUTHBERT'S CHAPEL
INNER FARNE

Visit the chapel between May and July and you'll have the joy of being surrounded not only by the sea but by hordes of Arctic terns, puffins and other seabirds whose ancestors may well have witnessed St Cuthbert's arrival on the island.

SPIRITUAL ORIENTATION
Roman Catholic/Ecumenical

PHYSICAL ORIENTATION
Inner Farne, Farne Islands, Northumberland NE68 7YT
Grid reference: NU 218 359
OS Landranger map 75

PUBLIC TRANSPORT
Although Chathill railway station is only 5 miles away from Seahouses, where there's a boat to Farne Island, it's simpler to take a train to Alnmouth station (virgintrainseastcoast.com; 03457 225111), walk half a mile to the roundabout at Lesbury, and hop on the X18 bus (arrivabus.co.uk; 0344 8004411) to Seahouses. Four companies offer trips that cross the 2 nautical miles of North Sea and land on Inner Farne – their ticket kiosks can be found on the harbour front: Billy Shiel MBE (farne-islands.com; 01665 720308), Golden Gate (farneislandsboattrips.co.uk; 01665 721210), Serenity (farneislandtours.co.uk; 01665 721667) and Hanvey's (farneislands.co.uk; 01665 720388). These sail in the summer and, at a much reduced frequency, in the autumn.

OPENING ARRANGEMENTS
Open whenever Inner Farne is open to visitors (end March to end October). The National Trust levies a charge for landing on the island. For further details see nationaltrust.org.uk.

SERVICES
Every year a few services are held in the chapel by sundry Christian groups.

eek out the Farne Islands on a map of Northumbria and they appear to be little more than a handful of pebbles tossed into the North Sea. Overshadowed by the much larger Holy Island to the north, their importance to the history of Christianity in Britain is often overlooked. The little chapel on the biggest island of the group, Inner Farne, is one of the few remaining physical links we have to the isle's monastic past.

As early as the year 640 we find St Aidan making his way here to get away from the hustle and bustle of Holy Island, where he served as a bishop. However, it was a former shepherd boy called Cuthbert who really made his mark on Inner Farne. The 39-year-old prior of Holy Island arrived in 676, intent on the life of a hermit, and had the good fortune of having angels help him build his cell. After a short spell as Bishop of Holy Island,

Cuthbert returned to Inner Farne to die in 687. The beautiful little 14th-century chapel, much restored in the 1800s, is dedicated to him, while the remains of his cell are believed to lie beneath the grand Castell Tower next door.

Although there were many others who came to live here after Cuthbert – including Bartholomew, who stayed from 1150 to 1193 and wrote the Farne Meditations – not all were quite so virtuous. The 15th century proved a particularly sticky patch in the life of the Benedictine monastery. John de Rypon was sent away for 'extravagance', John Harom was discovered to have pawned the chapel's chalice, and John Kirke was caught pursuing women.

The chapel is the only monastery building to have survived. However, just a few yards away the National Trust visitor centre is built upon the base of a twin

with its own farmland on the mainland and plentiful grey seals to eat. Thankfully, these were never driven to extinction and, with around 6,000 seals, today it is one of Europe's most important colonies.

However, it's not the seals you'll first notice on a trip to the chapel but the birdlife. Puffins (known locally as Tommy Noddies), guillemots, shags, cormorants, razorbills, eiders and numerous others make the 16 acres of Inner Farne their home. It is the Arctic terns though that make their presence most keenly felt to summer visitors to St Cuthbert's. Those pilgrims who forget their hats are obliged to cover their heads with whatever they have to hand as they scurry to the chapel. On their way they pass through a busy nesting area and the birds, fearful for the safety of their young, dive-bomb the heads of interlopers with some resolve.

It's fitting, given all this avian activity, that when St Cuthbert lived here he laid down decrees protecting the island's birdlife. They were possibly the first such regulations anywhere in the world. To this day, eiders are known in Northumberland as 'cuddy ducks' (from 'Cuthbert's ducks').

Having run the gauntlet, take a look at the stone coffin outside the chapel. It may well belong to Thomas Sparowe, who died in 1430 and was novice-master of the House of Farne, as the monastery was known. Pass through the ogee-headed doorway and you enter a dark world.

chapel, dedicated to St Mary. The Fishehouse [sic], whose remains moulder by the modern-day jetty, is on the site of a guesthouse St Cuthbert built for those coming to visit him. Despite the less than ecclesiastical behaviour of some of its inmates, the monastery flourished until Henry VIII had it dissolved in 1536.

By that time, the current St Cuthbert's chapel was just 166 years old, but as some of its stone is 12th- or 13th-century, presumably a building stood here before 1370. The monastery was prosperous,

At the western end are the remains of a galilee: a chapel or porch often found in churches with a St Cuthbert association. In the south wall the one original medieval window has been blocked up. Those that do let in a little light were renovated in Victorian times, the glass for the striking east window made by the Gateshead artist-glazier William Wailes in 1844. An abundance of dark wood compounds the gloom, while medieval grave slabs do nothing to lighten the mood.

Fortunately, the furnishings are so extraordinary that they are wont to lift the spirits, or at least give the visitor a start. In 1848, Archdeacon Thorp, who had taken it upon himself to restore St Cuthbert's, began to fill it with paraphernalia he had brought from Durham Cathedral and which had been made for Bishop Cosin in around 1665. Since the colossus at Durham is of a rather different scale to this humble island chapel, the theatrical Gothic stalls with their Baroque cherubim heads tend to dominate the space. They lord it over the pews and altar table, shipped in much later, and render the church somewhat claustrophobic.

Perhaps, in the end, it is what St Cuthbert would have wanted. After all, the cell he built here with the help of the angels had barely enough room for one. 🕮

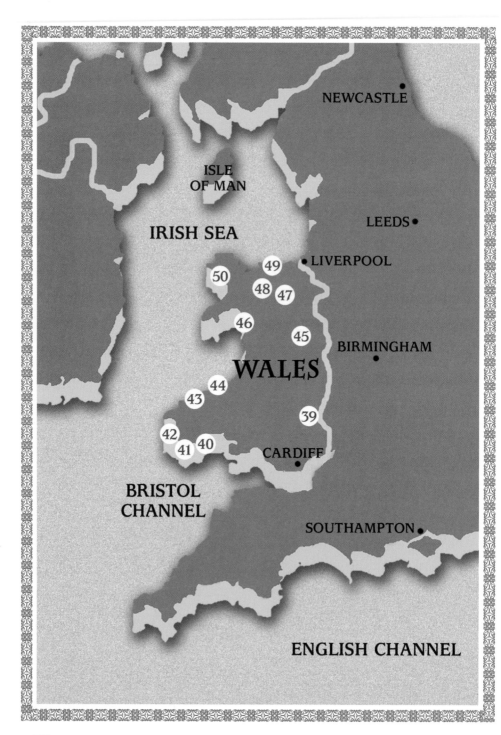

NEWCASTLE

ISLE
OF MAN

IRISH SEA

LEEDS

LIVERPOOL

50 49 48 47

46 45

BIRMINGHAM

WALES

44

43

39

42 41 40

CARDIFF

BRISTOL
CHANNEL

SOUTHAMPTON

ENGLISH CHANNEL

WALES

ST ISSUI'S
PATRICIO

The rare medieval rood loft and screen is one of the finest you'll see in Britain.

SPIRITUAL ORIENTATION
The Church in Wales

PHYSICAL ORIENTATION
Patricio, Crickhowell, Powys NP7 7LP
Grid reference: SO 278 224
OS Landranger map 161

PUBLIC TRANSPORT
From Abergavenny railway station (arrivatrainswales. co.uk; 0333 3211202) your best bet is to cycle the 8 miles to Patricio (often marked as 'Partrishow', the old form of the name), though the climb gets Tour de France steep as you approach the church and the bewildering network of roads is likely to have you scratching your head several times on the way. Alternatively, Abergavenny possesses a clutch of taxi companies.

OPENING ARRANGEMENTS
Open daily.

SERVICES
11.15am 1st & 3rd Sunday (Eucharist).

 visit to St Issui's in the Brecon Beacons offers the chance to take in not just one tiny place of worship but two. Since they are located in the remote and lofty hamlet of Patricio, this double helping of pleasure is certainly merited by the effort it takes to get there, particularly if you have arrived under your own steam. For reasons unknown, both somehow escaped the worst excesses of the Reformation, meaning that they have retained their three stone altars,

churchyard cross, instructive wall painting and magnificent rood loft and screen – one of the choicest examples in the land.

From the outside, the medieval church looks much like any other. Pass through the generous lychgate – which gives the appearance of having sheltered myriad generations of pall-bearers from the searing heat of the sun and the dismal ministrations of the rain but was actually only built in 1908 – and still nothing looks askew. Indeed, your attention may already

have wandered to the curious lean-to next to the church or the magnificent view down to your right of the lower Grwyne Fawr Valley. However, if you happen to walk through the first door you come to, rather than the one protected by the 14th-century porch, you do not enter the main church at all but a completely separate chapel with a history discrete from that of the church.

A common feature they do share is a dedication to St Issui, an early Celtic missionary who established a cell here by a sacred well. He was apparently much loved in his day and when he was foully murdered his cell became a place of pilgrimage.

Cured of his leprosy by the well water, an 11th-century pilgrim from the Continent gave a sum of gold to pay for the building of a church on the hillside above the well. It seems very likely that St Issui's Chapel is built on the site of that church. Indeed, the remains of St Issui might well have been buried where the stone altar now stands. This has six consecration crosses incised on it, which is one more than might be expected since they ordinarily represented the five wounds of Christ on the cross.

Above the altar, the square window, or squint, allowed those inside the chapel to look through to the church and thus join in when Mass was taken there. In a niche to the left stands a modern-day treasure: an aluminium statuette of St Issui created by Frank Roper in 1995. This replaced one destroyed 400 years earlier during the

Reformation. Drawing on Celtic sources, Roper has made a thing of rare beauty, deftly steering clear of giving Issui the look of extreme piety foisted onto most saints by their sculptors. Rather, Roper makes him seem a little world weary. This is a saint you could really warm to – you want to sit him down and give him a cup of tea.

The window in the chapel's west wall is 13th century, the north wall earlier still, but both the south wall and roof are 14th century, which strongly suggests these last two collapsed and were rebuilt, possibly in order to create a hermitage. Curiously, at the beginning of the 20th century the

church must have had a terrible sense of déjà vu because the south wall was within a whisker of falling down again and bringing the roof with it. This time, however, the eminent church architect William Caröe (see St Mary of the Angels, Brownshill, p134) was summoned. He had the wall underpinned and so saved the day. He didn't, however, save the chapel from the degradation of being used as a storeroom. It was only reconsecrated as recently as 1991.

The church next door is generally of a slightly later composition but, if anything, feels like the more venerable of the two. It

has two stone altars, a wonderfully creepy medieval painting of Time – a skeleton holding an hourglass and scythe – and a hulking great font from the mid-11th century, one of the oldest in Wales. Next to it is a chest carved from a single tree trunk. The valuables it stored could only be removed when the rector and two churchwardens each produced the key they kept to one of the three locks.

But it is the exquisite rood loft and screen that overwhelms all else. Possibly given as a gift by the Abbot of Llanthony Priory or a member of the local Herbert family, it was carved from Irish oak in the

15th century. The intricate tracery is very delicately worked, as is the dragon devouring a vine on the south corner of one of the beams. The loft would originally have been adorned with flowers and lit by numerous candles. Sadly, its creator is unknown – it has been variously suggested that it might have been a Flemish, an Italian or a Welsh craftsman.

Back outside, there is that peculiar stone lean-to. Once a stable for the priest's pony, there's a little fireplace inside so that, on wet days, his cloak could be dried while he preached. A medieval churchyard cross, partly destroyed during the

Reformation, has been updated with a tabernacle top featuring various figures including Archbishop Baldwin. He is believed to have preached a sermon urging support for the Third Crusade at this cross in 1188. It can be viewed from the comfort of a stone bench along the south wall.

After visiting the two St Issui's, there's a further treat in store. Walk back down the road to the first tight bend and you'll find some stone steps leading down to the very same well that drew St Issui here over 1,400 years ago.

ST DAVID'S
CALDEY ISLAND

The Tree of Life window proves that not all the best church art is necessarily ancient.

SPIRITUAL ORIENTATION
Cistercian

PHYSICAL ORIENTATION
Caldey Island, off Tenby, Pembrokeshire SA70 7UJ
Grid reference: SS 142 966
OS Landranger map 158

PUBLIC TRANSPORT
From Tenby railway station (arrivatrainswales.co.uk; 0333 3211202) it's a pleasant walk to the harbour from where Caldey Island kiosk sells tickets for sailings to Caldey on most days (but never Sunday) from mid-April to October. However, it doesn't take much of a wind for sailings to be cancelled, often for days at a time, so come prepared to be disappointed.

For information ring 01834 844453. NB This is the only boat that lands on Caldey.

OPENING ARRANGEMENTS
Open when the island itself is open for visitors (Monday to Saturday).

SERVICES
None.

 pleasure delayed is a pleasure doubled, as the old saw goes, and you might well find yourself being very delayed in crossing over to Caldey to see St David's. It only takes a breath of wind from the wrong quarter to make landing on the island impossible for the one boat that plies the route from the picturesque harbour.

Those who manage to make the voyage follow in the wake of a multitude of monks, the first of whom hazarded the short hop from mainland to island in the 6th century. The very first abbot was called Pyro and his name lives on in the Welsh name for Caldey, Ynys Bŷr ('Pyro's Island'). He was succeeded by an abbot named Samson who went on to sainthood. It was undeniably a promising start, but four centuries later the community came to a halt, probably due to pillaging carried out by Norse raiders.

The sound of plainsong only returned to the island in the 12th century, when a priory was established there by the black-habited Benedictine Tironensians of St Dogmaels Abbey in Pembrokeshire. On this occasion it was an enemy closer to home who proved the monastery's downfall, with Henry VIII dissolving it in 1536.

From the jetty on Caldey, it's an agreeable stroll along the road to the collection of buildings known as the

village. The roughly 500-acre island has a population of about 40, not including the monks. At the museum, a left turn will take you past the shining white walls of a 20th-century Arts and Crafts style abbey (the medieval priory, much of which has remained intact, lies further to the south). The road curves to the right where, on a little hillock just past the statue of St Samson, stands St David's church.

In the churchyard, beyond the rows of simple crosses marking the burial places of monks and residents of Caldey, there is a preaching cross designed in 1919 by John Coates Carter, the architect who was also responsible for the abbey. The scene looks relatively modern but this is the site of a burial ground that goes back to the days before even the first monks arrived, perhaps even 2,000 years ago. Pagan Celts viewed islands as a sort of stepping stone between earth and the afterlife and it's possible that corpses were even brought here from the mainland for interment.

The current building, which serves as the island's parish church, is an amalgam of Celtic, Norman, Victorian and early 20th-century work and used to be known as St Mary's by the Seashore, on account of the tidal inlet that once existed where the village stands today. The bulk of the structure is Norman but, like the

slow descent to ruination. For once, it was Victorians who came to the rescue. There were no monks on Caldey in the 19th century but the island landowners stepped in and restored the church, re-roofing it completely. It was left to the island's short-lived third wave of monks to install the stained-glass windows that are the glory of St David's.

The glaziers were a group of Anglican Benedictines who bought the whole island in 1906 and built the abbey that is now its most eye-catching feature. Unusually, seven years after they arrived on Caldey, they turned their backs on Anglicanism and became part of the Roman Catholic Church. Their tenure over the island did not last long, though, for they soon hit the rocks financially and in 1925 sold up and left. They were replaced four years later by Cistercian monks, or Trappists, from Scourmont Abbey in Belgium, the strict and contemplative order that still runs Caldey today. They support themselves by dint of dairy farming, perfumery, chocolaterie, shortbread-making and tourism (their success in this last field means it's unlikely you'll get St David's all to yourself).

The church is a simple nave and chancel, the two separated by a large and much restored arch. Its four Benedictine windows were designed and created by Dom Theodore Bailey. Two are formed of two lights: 'The Two Davids' has the

churchyard, its roots are much older. Its foundations were dug out by 6th-century monks for a chapel they constructed here, presumably choosing the spot because of the presence of the Pagan graveyard. It's even possible that some sections of the nave walls are leftovers from that same chapel. Unfortunately, once the monastery was closed down, the church began its

patron saint of Wales next to King David of Old Testament fame, while the other shows a Madonna and Child next to St Helena. Meanwhile, the Fish window is a modern twist on one of the earliest known Christian symbols. However, Bailey's greatest triumph is the Tree of Life window. Dominated by blues and purples, the tree actually appears to be three trees.

It has been suggested that they represent the three crosses on Calvary, but given the window's title it's not unreasonable to suggest that they symbolise the Holy Trinity. It's something to ponder as you make your way back across the island – one that has been enticing people to make the short trip from the mainland since before the Holy Trinity was even a phrase.

41 ST GOVAN'S CHAPEL
BOSHERSTON

The chapel's setting is truly spine-tingling: jammed incongruously into cliffs on a remote section of coastline.

SPIRITUAL ORIENTATION
Roman Catholic

PHYSICAL ORIENTATION
nr Bosherston, Pembrokeshire SA71 5DR
Grid reference: SR 966 929
OS Landranger map 158

PUBLIC TRANSPORT
From Pembroke railway station (arrivatrainswales.co.uk; 0333 3211202) take the 388 bus (silcoxcoaches.co.uk; 01646 683143) to the Coastguard Station in Bosherston, from where it's just over a mile's walk through the Castlemartin firing range to the chapel.

OPENING ARRANGEMENTS
Always open, though access to it is occasionally barred by activity at the Castlemartin firing range. Check firing times at milfordmarina.com/castlemartin-range-1.

SERVICES
None.

f ever a chapel were weighed down by myths and legends, many of them of rare inanity, it is poor old St Govan's. Its extraordinary location – perched halfway down a cliff beside a holy well – combined with its genesis at a time so distant that actual facts about it were always going to be in short supply made it inevitable that people would fill in the gaps with fables, folklore and miraculous happenings.

It's probably best to get these out of the way first before mining for the truth. They begin even before you enter this tiny building wedged into the Pembrokeshire coastline. The descent to the chapel with its diminutive cell beyond includes a plethora of half steps and indeterminate little drops, a circumstance that has led to a belief that it is impossible for 'mortal man' to count the same number of steps up as they counted down.

Govan's very first moments here are said to have involved a miraculous event. In attempting to throw off some pirates, the saint hid in a crevice in the cliffs. The rocks closed around him until the pirates had gone past, when they opened again. Some indentations in a boulder are said to date from that incident, having been made when the saint laid his hand upon it. Likewise, fissures in a cleft were made by his ribs while he lay concealed. Various authorities attest to the certainty of wishes being granted to those who can turn around within this fracture. Meanwhile, the

squirrelled it away inside the large boulder just outside the chapel (now known as the Bell Rock). When he tapped the rock the bell would ring out a thousand times louder than it had before, which, if true, must have left him with permanently perforated eardrums and almost certain tinnitus.

Finally, some fanciful folk would have you believe that the man we know as St Govan was really King Arthur's nephew Sir Gawain. It's no wonder that Govan became the patron saint of the gullible.

spot where the altar now stands is purported to be Govan's burial place.

The waters from a spring situated just inside the chapel entrance could apparently cure various eye and skin complaints as well as rheumatism, properties also ascribed to a larger well (now dry) outside the chapel. Indeed, the water there seems to have been imbued with even greater medicinal powers because the halt and the lame are said to have left their crutches there as an offering, having walked away cured of their disabilities.

We are assured that the bell that once graced the now empty bell-cote can be heard tolling mournfully from its resting place out on the sea bed, presaging the imminent doom of a vessel in those waters. Another bell, this time a silver one, is alleged to have been given to the saint only to be purloined by pirates. When it was retrieved (by angels, naturally), Govan

But enough. What we do know of the man is that he grew up in County Wexford in Ireland in the early part of the 6th century and his name was probably actually spelled Gobhan, meaning 'smith'. He joined the monastery of Dairinis in Wexford, possibly starting in the kitchens. Along with two others, he was sent to Rome by the monastery's founder, St Ailbe, to bring back an accurate form of the Mass. He eventually became abbot at Dairinis and then, as an old man, made his life-changing trip to Wales. His motives for sailing across the Irish Sea are not known, though it's been posited that he might have been engaged in a bit of mapmaking.

The pursuit by pirates is feasible for they were known to be at large in those seas at that time and a fully fledged abbot would have made a juicy kidnapping target. The coast of the Castlemartin

peninsula would also have offered up plenty of hiding places in the event of a chase. However he got here, Govan does seem to have built a cell in these cliffs and spent the rest of his life in it, dying here in 586.

The chapel that bears his name is a simple nave measuring roughly 17ft by 12ft, with an opening leading to a rough cell beyond. The age of the current structure is a source of contention, though that it was built somewhere between the 11th and 13th centuries seems likely, with an original chapel built by St Govan's followers in the 6th century a possibility.

Inside, the chapel appears to be merely an empty shell of rough stones, green with mould. However, once your eyes have adjusted to the gloom, features begin to emerge. There's the opening for the spring down on the floor, with a long bench or shelf and aumbry nearby; a piscina and a small niche in the south wall; a circle marked in plasterwork on the west wall, possibly with a '6' and an '0' inside it; while at the east end there is a plain stone altar and a few steps that lead up to the small rocky enclosure or cell.

Pass through the doorway in the west wall to explore the remainder of the elderly St Govan's domain. The well he used there has run dry, and any curative qualities its waters might once have had have been lost. Happily, the tranquillity found in this place – facing the open sea but tucked away from the world – is still balm for the soul. 🦋

42 SEAMEN'S CHAPEL
ANGLE

Look out for the charming reredos depicting local scenes from a bygone age.

SPIRITUAL ORIENTATION
The Church in Wales

PHYSICAL ORIENTATION
St Mary's churchyard, Angle, Pembrokeshire SA71 5AR
Grid reference: SM 866 029
OS Landranger map 157/158

PUBLIC TRANSPORT
From Pembroke railway station (arrivatrainswales.co.uk; 0333 3211202), the 388 bus (silcoxcoaches.co.uk; 01646 683143) will show you all the sights of this lovely corner of Pembrokeshire before depositing you at last in Angle, some 1hr 20 minutes later.

OPENING ARRANGEMENTS
Open daily during daylight hours.

SERVICES
None.

t says something about the peculiar precariousness of a life on the ocean wave that over the centuries a goodly number of chapels have been created around the coast of Britain so that seamen might pray for deliverance from the vicissitudes of the seas, or have their mortal remains rest there a while if their prayers were not answered. Many of these became ordinary churches but the one in Angle is something of a rarity: not only does it remain a dedicated seamen's chapel, it is actually set in the graveyard of another, much larger, church. Unless you decided to explore the churchyard, you might easily visit St Mary's in Angle and never notice the steeply gabled little building that hides behind it.

The church of St Mary's is believed to have been built in the 13th or 14th century, making it slightly older than the Seamen's Chapel, and may well have replaced an older place of worship. The village the two sanctuaries serve used to be known as Nangle – a corruption of *in angulo*, the Latin phrase meaning 'in a corner' – but somewhere along the line the 'N' fell off (this happens more often than you might suppose: for example, an apron used to be called a napron). The angle in question is a sharp bend in the coastline that provided an ideal shelter for boats at the seaward end of the Milford Haven estuary. For many hundreds of years the people here lived by fishing (with a little farming thrown in – medieval strip fields are still in evidence) and doubtless many an anxious hour has been spent in the tiny chapel interceding for those caught out in Atlantic storms.

The building was erected by Edward de Shirburn, a Knight of Nangle, in 1447, possibly as a charnel chapel of ease for sailors. A plaque above the door declares that it is dedicated to St Anthony, without specifying which St Anthony that might be (there were at least three by that time). Enquiries into the matter have all drawn a blank, so you can take your pick.

Parked in a forlorn corner of the churchyard, with a smattering of graves around it and a rookery above, this grey stone box with its windowless western face combines the proportions of a Wendy house with an undeniably mournful air. However, once you have climbed the short set of steps and passed through the plain arched doorway, matters begin to improve considerably.

Just inside the door to the right there is an effigy of a man lying somewhat casually on the floor, as if taking a little nap. It is thought that this is Edward de Shirburn himself. Behind the wooden altar rail, which is actually more of a fence, stands an undecorated stone altar. If the tiles in front of it look familiar, it probably means you have just come from St David's Cathedral because the pattern is the same as used there. There's a minute triangular niche to the right that might once have been an aumbry but is now the home of a red-headed angel pouring a cup of tea. A lobster pot on the other side of the altar

adds to the slight air of kitsch. Nine chairs just about fill the nave, on one of which can be found an old litany for seafarers mounted on a board that has split in two (an event the more superstitious mariner would surely take as an ill omen).

There are two stained-glass windows, both featuring apposite subjects for a seamen's chapel. One references the miracle of the calming of the waves, showing the moment the disciples wake Jesus because their boat is in danger. The other contains a second sea-based miracle. A brightly garbed Jesus walks on the water towards the disciples, who are fishing from a boat. Peter has just stepped over the side to meet him but has begun to sink. The words he cries out – 'Lord, help me or I perish' – appear underneath and will doubtless have been repeated in some form or other by many a seaman.

The real gem of the chapel is its recently restored reredos, a screen at the back of the altar. It features a statuette of a crucified Christ dressed in the robes of the Order of Melchizedek, clothing that symbolises his eternal priesthood. He presides over a bucolic depiction of Angle. A pair of golden angels look down on fishermen launching their golden boat, on a farmer holding a golden scythe, on golden-horned cattle and docile sheep, on children chasing butterflies with a golden net, on a golden St Mary's with a golden Seamen's Chapel playing peek-a-boo behind it, and on a golden sailing ship heading out to sea.

It is left to the chapel crypt to testify to a less glistering side of life here. Up to the beginning of the 20th century, this was where the bodies of seamen and others who were washed ashore were kept prior

to burial (distressingly, many of them were never identified). They sleep outside in the churchyard along with a group of young servicemen laid to rest to the side of the chapel. The latter group were all killed in action in the two World Wars and count among their number three Canadians and a Czech.

Other local men died rather less honourably when, on 30 January 1894, the sailing ship *Loch Shiel* struck nearby Thorn Island during a storm, thus precipitating Angle's very own *Whisky Galore!* episode. Though the crew was saved by three brave lifeboatmen, the cargo of 7,000 cases of Scotch was deposited onto the rocks. A father and son were swept away attempting to retrieve some of the booty. Another man expired later having simply drunk himself to death, which was not perhaps the form of spirit-filled existence the chapel sought to encourage.

CHURCH OF THE HOLY CROSS
MWNT

The glorious sight of Mwnt church, nestling in the lee of a grassy knoll with Cardigan Bay behind, is one to lift the spirits.

SPIRITUAL ORIENTATION
The Church in Wales

PHYSICAL ORIENTATION
Mwnt, Ferwig, Ceredigion SA43 1QH
Grid reference: SN 195 520
OS Landranger map 145

PUBLIC TRANSPORT
There's no public transport to Mwnt – the closest you can get is Cardigan, a town 4 miles away. To get there, take a train to Carmarthen station (arrivatrainswales.co.uk; 0333 3211202) then a 460 bus (richardbros.co.uk; 01239 613756) from the bus station to Cardigan. From there it's a bracing walk on country roads or a taxi.

OPENING ARRANGEMENTS
Open daily.

SERVICES
6pm Sunday (Evening Worship) throughout July and August
9.30am Easter Day (Holy Communion)
9pm Christmas Eve (Holy Communion)
All services are in Welsh and English.

There are few churches in Britain that enjoy such a fortunate setting as Mwnt. Sheltered by a conical hill from the big open skies above it, the building sits on a glorious greensward that rushes towards the cliffs. Behind it, the waters of Cardigan Bay glint and glisten or froth and foam as the weather dictates. With its black slate roof and sparkling white walls, the little church makes quite a statement in a scene otherwise dominated by emeralds and sapphires.

For centuries, the hearts of pilgrims have been lifted by this sight at they made their way between St David's and Bardsey Island. In the Middle Ages they would have found a land well populated with fishermen and their families. Today, aside from the odd farmhouse, there is little here but one or two flocks of sheep spread liberally across large fields, and one or two flocks of static caravans packed tightly into smaller ones. In the summer months day-trippers flock here too, squeezing their cars down the narrow roads, attracted by the church and the National Trust-owned beach below it.

A place of worship is said to have stood here from the very earliest days of Christianity in Britain although no physical evidence has been found to support this.

However, the church's dedication to the Holy Cross is one that was popular in the very early medieval period. In this case it is a reference to a tall stone cross that is believed to have stood guard on top of Foel y Mwnt, the hillock that rises directly behind the church. The date of the current building is difficult to ascertain but it may well be 13th or 14th century.

The terrain where it has been built is not quite flat and so it appears to be gripping on to the lower slopes in a bid not to slide even further down them. A photograph from 1912 on display inside shows the church sporting a startling toothpaste-white roof as well, which gives it a ghostly air. On taking a second glance at the picture you almost expect the building to have mysteriously disappeared.

Before entering the church, take a look at the well-weathered gravestones in the little churchyard. There you will find two centenarians and a nonagenarian among other long-lived parishioners. The locals were walking adverts for the benefits of bracing sea breezes and their longevity led to them being called Hen Gewri'r Mwnt (the Old Giants of Mwnt).

Their bones rest perhaps a little more easily than certain others to be found in the vicinity. In 1155, a band of Flemish soldiers sailed from Flanders and landed

at Mwnt. They were met by a force of Welshmen who defeated them soundly. Well into the 20th century it was not uncommon for the remains of one or other of the vanquished Flemings to be unearthed in the farmland about the church or on the beach below.

The interior of the building is not in any way fanciful and it's unsurprising to learn that during the great Methodist Revival (see Milldale Chapel, p159) clergy of a Wesleyan bent found a warm reception here. Beneath whitewashed walls, ranks of orderly pews face a simple altar and pulpit illuminated by an unremarkable two-light trefoiled window.

A squat little stone font sits by the entrance. This may date from the 12th century and so be older than the church itself. Mullioned windows in the north wall, while lacking in stained glass, are filled with the green and blue of the hill and the sky.

It is the abundance of flowers often found here that really brings joy to the eye. On occasions it seems that almost every horizontal surface has been given some floral adornment. The plinth of the font, the harmonium, the window sills and the table holding the inevitable picture postcards are all embellished with charming little arrangements, while the

altar is frequently bedecked with a positive river of flowers.

The church's most intriguing feature is a short flight of stone steps in the north wall of the nave, nearly all that remains of a 15th-century rood loft, a platform supported by a rood screen (which is also missing). At one time it seems to have been decorated with the heads of the 12 Apostles. Three small sections of the loft have been attached to the wall above the harmonium and it's possible to make out a design of trailing roses running across them. Originally the whole affair would have been painted and gilded, and though these remaining pieces may not look much, they excited church historians when they were discovered because such a pattern had not been seen before on rood lofts from that period. In truth, it doesn't take much to excite a church historian.

On the north side of the chancel, a little niche (also trimmed with flowers) provides a more complete, if heart-rending, window on the medieval world. This was once a literal window installed so that lepers and others banished from the church during Holy Communion could at least look in and see the altar. What comfort this gave them as the wicked sea winds came whipping about them, we shall never know.

ST INA'S
LLANINA

In spring, the setting of this modest little church is made even more picturesque by garlands of bluebells.

SPIRITUAL ORIENTATION
The Church in Wales

PHYSICAL ORIENTATION
Llanina, New Quay,
Ceredigion SA45 9SH
Grid reference: SN 404 598
OS Landranger map 145/146

PUBLIC TRANSPORT
From Aberystwyth railway station (arrivatrainswales.co.uk; 0333 3211202) make the short walk to the town's bus station to board the T5 bus to the Cambrian Hotel just east of New Quay. From there it's a 0.5-mile walk to the chapel along a picturesque minor road. After going over a bridge, the church gate is immediately to your right, opposite the entrance to Llanina woods.

OPENING ARRANGEMENTS
Always open.

SERVICES
2.30pm every Sunday
1st, 3rd & 5th Sunday (Holy Communion)
2nd & 4th Sunday (Evensong).

here's something very ancient about the approach to St Ina's. A long meandering and narrow lane penetrates woodland that keeps it in deep shadow even on a bright summer's day. Below it, cutting itself a slender valley, a brook pushes its way through the trees. From time to time the road, with a sigh, collapses into the little gully its companion has made. It's easy to imagine medieval pilgrims trudging along here in their jerkins and smocks, carrying firkins of small beer and stocks of dried fish to sustain themselves on their journey.

What sort of church they found in the clearing in the woods is impossible to say because the current St Ina's is not only the result of rebuilding works carried out in 1850 (and a restoration in 1905) but it is at least the third church that has stood here and may even be the seventh. Looking at it through the arched gateway that pierces the graveyard's stone wall, the building actually appears slightly older than it is. A solid narrow box of sombre grey stone, the roof supports a little crenellated bell-cote that leans over the end of the roof as if to see who might be going through the door below. Only the tidy slates and modern guttering suggest that the bell-cote hasn't been keeping an eye on the congregation for all that long.

Of even more recent fabrication is the arrow-straight concrete-slab path that gives

the churchyard the look of a 1970s recreation ground. Thankfully, this is compensated for by a tantalising glimpse of the Irish Sea beyond the church, and a clutch of slate gravestones by the door inscribed in Welsh. Being very thin, a few of these have begun to fracture and thus, like the church, look rather older than the 160-odd years they've racked up guarding the bones of the faithful. Little droppings and scrapings around them betray the presence of rabbits, no doubt foraging from their burrows along the shore.

That same shore has played a crucial role in the life of the church and may even have been responsible for it being here at all. The story goes that King Ina of Wessex was shipwrecked nearby. He was saved by some local people who proceeded to take care of him and his crew. Some time later he returned and built a church in grateful recognition of the kindness he received here. A somewhat similar tale crops up in the history of Llangwyfan (p255) and several other coastal churches, but that's not to say that this one has no foundation. However, if the king did establish a church here it has long since been lost to the sea, which over the centuries has chewed off great chunks of this coastline.

St Ina (also spelt St Ine) is very little known now but he was quite the man in his day. He reigned over Wessex for nearly four decades from 688 to 726, and despite losing the parts of southeast England he had inherited from his father Cædwalla, he founded both Wells Cathedral and Glastonbury Abbey, and codified the West Saxons' first ever set of laws. He eventually abdicated the throne in order to make a pilgrimage to Rome with his wife, Ethelburga (not the Ethelburga of Great Givendale, p174). As happened to a number of pre-Norman British kings, he went on to be canonised.

At first glance, indeed at second glance, the interior of St Ina's can seem a tad disappointing because its Elizabethan decor is very much from the second Elizabeth's reign. The church is carpeted from wall to wall with a thick, plush and spotlessly clean royal blue carpet on which stand neat rows of modern chairs fitted with matching padded seats and backs.

This is a place in which a maundering preacher can be endured in some comfort.

However, take a third glance and you'll notice a few features to pique your interest. The first is the stone octagonal font. Covered with a smart modern cap, it is clearly of a much greater age than the current church and was presumably rescued from a previous incarnation.

Another survivor is a diamond-shaped dedication to a former vicar of Llanina and noted satirical bard, John Lloyd, who is buried beneath the chancel. Above his last resting place, a stained-glass window installed in 1943 depicts a fittingly coastal episode from the life of Christ. Finally, crossing the nave is an oak beam with a vine carved on it. Depending on the degree of romance in your soul, this is either a section from a 15th-century rood screen or a fragment of a ship that foundered off Llanina Point.

John Lloyd was not the only satirical bard who knew St Ina's. In the late 1930s, at the invitation of Lord Howard de Walden, Dylan Thomas spent time writing at Plas Llanina, the mansion next door. However, one imagines he passed more time in the local pub than in the church.

Although the beach appears to begin where the churchyard ends, it is separated from it by the final moments of the River Llethi. Fortunately, once you've had your fill of St Ina's, you can reach the strand via the Wales Coast Path, there to lose yourself in quiet contemplation of the waters from which the plucky locals plucked the king. 🦋

FRIENDS MEETING HOUSE
DOLOBRAN

This simple place of worship imparts an extraordinary sense of detachment from time as well as place.

SPIRITUAL ORIENTATION
Religious Society of Friends (Quakers)

PHYSICAL ORIENTATION
Dolobran Isaf, Pontrobert, Meifod, Powys SY22 6HU
Grid reference: SJ 123 124
OS Landranger map 125

PUBLIC TRANSPORT
From Welshpool railway station (arrivatrainswales. co.uk; 0333 3211202), walk to the High Street where you can catch a bus for either Pontrobert or Meifod. For the former, take the 87 to Heniarth Bridge followed by the 73 (both owenstravel. co.uk; 01691 652126); for the latter you merely need to hop on the 76. The Glyndŵr's Way long distance footpath runs between these two villages and right past the back of the meeting house. It's roughly a mile from Pontrobert and just over a couple of miles from Meifod.

OPENING ARRANGEMENTS
Ring Sophie or Simon Meade in advance to arrange a visit (01938 500746 or 07990 622892).

SERVICES
10.30am Sunday
For further information see quaker.org.uk/meetings/ dolobran.

Amble across the low hills near Pontrobert in mid-Wales and you'll come across what appears to be a brick-built cottage charmingly situated in a little copse between fields. It certainly doesn't give the impression of being a church, and that is just as it should be because the Religious Society of Friends – to whom this building belongs – does not think of its places of worship as churches, hence the designation 'meeting house'.

Even up close, the scene remains entirely domestic. A trio of planks span a rivulet that runs below a well-kept garden complete with shed. The only indication that this is not simply a pleasant little dwelling somewhat lost in time is a small wooden sign hung over the gate by means of a couple of strips of wire that bears the words 'Friends Meeting House'.

Built at the turn of the 18th century, Dolobran is believed to be the oldest Quaker meeting house in Wales. However, its story goes back even further, to 1657. It was in that year, on the death of his father, that successful businessman Charles Lloyd returned home to the Dolobran estate where his family had lived for generations. There he witnessed the end of the

Commonwealth and the Restoration of the Monarchy. He also heard the preaching of Quaker evangelists who found Wales to be fertile soil for their teachings. Lloyd's subsequent conversion to Quakerism did not best please his family, or indeed the state, which locked him up, along with his wife and brother, for 10 years.

When they were finally released, thanks to the Declaration of Indulgence of 1672, they found the family home had been looted and all their livestock stolen.

Lloyd's son, also called Charles and also a member of the Friends, eventually took over what was left of the estate, which, despite the depredations visited upon it, was still at the heart of Quaker life (and indeed death, for there was a Quaker burial ground on estate land). However, meetings were still conducted in the houses of members and there was a yearning to have a place dedicated to such assemblies. Consequently, in 1699 a subscription was taken up, with eight

acknowledgement of their religious rights did afford them a degree of protection from persecution, though some abuses continued throughout the century.

The building has changed remarkably little since those times. It still has two front doors: the one on the right gives onto the meeting room while the one on the left allows access to a very simple cottage. The dwelling comprises little more than a kitchen downstairs (the oven installed in 1780 is so huge it bulges out into the meeting room next door) and some space to sleep upstairs. This side was also used for meetings held by Dolobran's women and as an overspill facility – you can still see where four removable panels were inserted to allow communication between the cottage and the meeting room.

The right-hand doorway tells its own story. It is large enough for two doors, yet only one is in place, indicating that there was a change of plan midway through the construction. The excellent potted history of the meeting house by Bron Roberts suggests that settling for a single door meant that a window could be placed further from the corner of the building, thus allowing a small gallery to be constructed. Look inside and there is still a gallery in place, albeit a modern version, the panels of the original one having been bought by some of William Penn's American descendants as reminders of their Welsh Quaker roots.

Friends donating a total of £31.10s. This small sum was supplemented by voluntary labour and the first meeting in the new building was held in April 1701. Such was the Friends' impatience to gather there that this took place even though the structure had no roof. Their eagerness was perhaps spurred by the awareness that their meeting house was not only a place to gather but also a physical sign that their particular form of Christianity was now recognised by the state. This official

The meeting house is laid out in the traditional Friends manner. There is no altar or pulpit and the benches are placed around three sides of the room with a small table and a rug in the middle. It has something of the appearance of a schoolroom, which was indeed one of the purposes it served. Shortly after the meeting house opened, money was raised to pay a teacher. An 18-year-old called James Kelsall took the post and taught here for 13 years, living in the adjoining cottage with his wife and children.

However, the course of Dolobran, and for that matter of Welsh Quakerism, did not run smooth. Large numbers of Friends emigrated to Pennsylvania, thus lowering attendances at the meeting house. Furthermore, the estate was struggling

financially and was eventually sold. The last regular meetings of this phase of Dolobran's life were held in 1780.

A century later, the estate was bought by one Samuel Sampson Lloyd, who allowed it to become a refuge for cattle. The building might well have crumbled away completely were it not for a Quaker couple called Mr and Mrs Edwards, who, while holidaying in the area in 1955, recognised the meeting house for what it was. At their bidding, the owner of the estate, Sampson Lloyd, leased it back to the Friends. Meetings began again in 1975 and are held each Sunday. Tucked away in a little crevice in the landscape and with no roads nearby, at Dolobran the silence and stillness that Friends meetings are renowned for are given full rein. 🦋

46 ST TANWG'S
LLANDANWG

A colossal gravestone from the 5th century is a fitting feature in what may be the oldest surviving Christian site in Britain.

SPIRITUAL ORIENTATION
The Church in Wales

PHYSICAL ORIENTATION
Llandanwg, Harlech, Gwynedd LL46 2SD
Grid reference: SH 568 282
OS Landranger map 124

PUBLIC TRANSPORT
From Llandanwg railway station (arrivatrainswales.co.uk; 0333 3211202) walk 0.3 miles down the road to the church, which is at the end of the road.

OPENING ARRANGEMENTS
Usually open daily during daylight hours. If locked, enquire at the neighbouring Y Maes Café (01341 241387).

SERVICES
6.30pm Sunday ('Celtic style') end of May to mid-September
6.30pm 3rd Sunday (Contemplative) September to May
3pm August Bank Holiday Sunday (Outdoor 'Hymns on the Maes' with Harlech Silver Band)
For further details see facebook.com/Llandanwg or ring parish administrator Pam Odam (01766 780030) or churchwarden John Adams (01341 241269).

h, poor St Tanwg's. 'I have come too late,' you may say to yourself as you approach, 'for the church has been buried up to its eaves in a sand dune.' In one respect you would be right, too. When the roof collapsed in the late 1800s the church did indeed fill with sand and only a public outcry led to it being dug out a year later. Even today the western half of the building is only separated from the grass-covered dune that threatens it by a narrow passage and a semicircular clearing by the door where headstones have been pressed into service as barriers against the encroaching beach.

The church is a simple stone construction dating from medieval times, though it's gone through a good number of changes since. It is said to have been built on the site of a church established by St Tanwg himself, possibly using stones from the beach. An obscure saint, Tanwg is very likely to have been one of the many missionaries sent by St Patrick from Ireland to Wales in the 5th century. Llandanwg (pronounced llan-dan-og) may be an inconsequential settlement nowadays but back then it was an important communications hub. Not only did it provide the safest haven for shipping

on the northwest Welsh coast, it was also served by Roman, Celtic and Bronze Age roads that afforded relatively easy access to both the Dee and the Severn rivers. If St Tanwg did establish a church here in about 435, as seems very probable, it may make this place the oldest surviving Christian outpost in all of Britain, which is quite a thought.

Ducking through the stone lychgate, the east wall contains a three-light rectangular window that very obviously replaced a much larger arched predecessor. If you trace the line of the sandstone arch down to the left you'll come to a curly-headed gent who turns out to be Edward III, the man who kicked off

the Hundred Years War with France. He is balanced on the right-hand side by a sadly less complete Philippa of Hainault, his wife and queen. Beneath them, in a large chest tomb, lies the poet Sion Phillips. He lived on nearby Shell Island and unfortunately drowned in 1620 while crossing from his home to Llandanwg at the age of 77.

Rather unexpectedly, as you make your way around to the entrance door at the far end of the church, you walk over a bit of old Manchester. The granite sets of the pathway were lifted from the streets of Britain's dampest city and laid here in 2008. Just above the door and to the right there is purportedly a stone inscribed with

a pre-Norman cross and some 17th-century graffiti, but if you can spot it consider your life's work to be pretty much complete. The bell tower is early medieval but the bell within was brought from Co. Sligo in Ireland in 1922 after years of service calling farm workers to their labours.

An excellent step-by-step guide available inside the church walks you through its salient points, both outside and in. It's particularly good in pointing out those parts of the building that have largely disappeared, leaving only the barest traces. This is true of the gallery that was destroyed when the roof

collapsed in 1883, and the rood screen, of which all that remains is a single beam. The latter was part of a scheme undertaken in the 14th century that nearly doubled the length of the church and added wall paintings (since destroyed), a choir loft and, most intriguingly, an oak-panelled canopy over the altar that bore images of the Devil and the Apostles. The 17th century saw the moving of various windows and the door, and the construction of the ill-fated gallery. In 1840, after around 1,400 years of service as the parish church of Harlech, St Tanwg's was supplanted by a second St Tanwg's, located in the town itself. The ancient church was plundered for items with which to furnish the new church, so if you want to inspect the 15th-century font, for example, you'll have to visit Harlech.

Despite this, there's still more than enough to see in this atmospheric tunnel-like structure. Long dark pews fill the nave, a reflection of the exposed roof beams above. Until recently, the Huchenfeld Cross, which was given as a token of reconciliation between Germany and Britain, sat in a corner near the altar table. Sadly, it has been removed to prevent it from being stolen. However, arrayed around the floor, in the splash of light that illuminates the chancel, are some impressively ancient stones. They include part of a 9th-century Celtic cross, a couple of 6th-century engraved stones,

one bearing the word 'Equestrinomine' ('by the name of Equester'), and a quern stone. This last relic, thought to have come from a burial chamber in Dyffryn Ardudwy, is a bowl in which grain was crushed. Since the 1840-sanctioned looting of St Tanwg's, it has been pressed into service at christenings. This must make the 4,000-year-old stone one of the oldest fonts in the world.

However, the cream of the crop is a stone with just a single decipherable word on it. This is a pillar gravestone – it's over 8ft long and weighs three-quarters of a ton. It was quarried in either Ireland or Anglesey and was carved in the 5th century. If you want to be transported back to the church that St Tanwg built here, then gaze on this, for it is a stone that stood in the graveyard when the church was still new. It commemorates a man about whom we know scarcely anything beyond his first name, carved over 1,500 years ago: Ingenvus.

RUG CHAPEL
CORWEN

The sheer overpowering flounciness of Rug Chapel's interior is a thing of joy.

SPIRITUAL ORIENTATION
Private chapel (Cadw)

PHYSICAL ORIENTATION
nr Corwen, Denbighshire
LL21 9BT
Grid reference: SJ 064 438
OS Landranger map 125

PUBLIC TRANSPORT
From Ruabon railway station
(arrivatrainswales.co.uk;
0333 3211202) take the
T3 bus from outside the
Wynnstay Arms Hotel to
Pont Corwen on the A5,
from where it's a mile-long
walk if you follow the
by-road after the bridge to
avoid a hike along the A5.
Alternatively, board the no.
94 bus from the same stop
to the Ty'n-y-Llidiart
industrial estate in Clawdd
Poncen, from where it's just
under a mile to the chapel.

OPENING ARRANGEMENTS
April to October inclusive,
Monday to Friday 10am–
5pm (with very occasional
exceptions)
Admission charged. Further
info at cadw.gov.wales.

SERVICES
None.

olonel William Salusbury was a man who clung courageously to the credo that, regardless of whatever evidence might stare him in the face, when it came to church decor, 'more is more'. His private chapel is a joyous denial of restraint in the pursuit of an ever higher 'High Church' look. His creation would have made a fitting venue for his coronation as the King of Bling.

The likely fate of the English king might have been on his mind when he built the chapel. In 1637, when craftsmen were feverishly bringing the 57-year-old colonel's designs to reality, the nation was riven with tensions and in just five years'

time would be torn apart by civil war. An ardent Royalist, William Salusbury's chapel represents a lusty two-fingered salute to the Puritanism of the Parliamentarians and all their spartan ways.

Had you seen Salusbury (sometimes spelt Salesbury) in his youth, it is unlikely you would have gambled a large amount on him dying peacefully at a great old age. He began life as a pirate (or 'privateer' as the British euphemistically put it), which might explain his attachment to glitz. This proved no bar to getting on in society and he became an MP briefly, fought bravely and well for Charles I as governor of Denbigh Castle, and wrote highly regarded

Welsh religious poetry. He died in 1660, living just long enough to see his beloved monarchy restored.

From the outside, the chapel looks extremely dull. It's a simple rectangle of roughly dressed stone with an obviously more recent vestry tacked on the side and a roof capped with a bell-cote and a modest cross at either end.

Once you enter the chapel, however, prepare to gasp. The trick here is to look upwards, for most of the many treasures Colonel Salusbury left us are to be found in the roof and the gallery. Every last inch of wood appears to have some carving or other upon it, putting one in mind of a person who has had their entire body tattooed. Foliage smothers every beam, leaving room only for some red-rose and white-rose motifs, sundry other flowers, a large 'IHS' (an abbreviation for the name of Jesus) and a '1637' at the east end. Stars shine in the upper heavens above the chancel, while below them rank upon rank of angels stare fixedly upon the altar. They are supported by two more carved angels that hover either side of the east window and yet more angels atop a complicated candelabrum. High on both sides of the nave, richly decorated panels overload the eye with their brightly coloured imagery.

The gallery that fills out the western end boasts a wonderful carved and painted balustrade which also affords visitors the welcome opportunity to take a closer look at the roof.

Back on terra firma, seek out the 17th-century painting of a recumbent skeleton accompanied by a pair of burning candles, a sundial, a skull and an hourglass – an illustration whose meaning is all too clear even to those who cannot read its Welsh and Latin inscriptions.

Salusbury fitted out the chapel with benches whose ends are carved with all manner of mythical creatures. The seating is completed by two rather extraordinary canopied pews that flank the altar – the sort of luxurious touch that would send a God-fearing Puritan apoplectic.

Infuriatingly, if inevitably, the chapel did not come through the Victorian era unscathed. In 1854–55, its then owner Robert Vaughan carried out some 'renovations'. The most noticeable of these is the mock-Jacobean wooden screen that divides the chancel from the nave. All the window glass was removed and stained-glass windows inserted in their stead. The west wall was remodelled, a small vestry added, backs were added to the bench seats to turn them into respectable pews, the floor was tiled and the doorway at the west end replaced. Aside from that, Vaughan left the place untouched.

The windows are a particularly unfortunate intrusion. The main three-light affair behind the altar looks like the winner in a competition to cram the most people into a stained-glass window. The only detail in any of the windows likely to have met with Salusbury's approval, given

the colonel's evident predilection for winged messengers, is the (it must be said, somewhat unexpected) scene depicting an angel in conference with Pilate's wife. The latter, looking suspiciously young, confides, 'I have suffered many things because of him.' It's probably true that behind every hand-washing statesman is a wronged woman but her complaint is still a bit rich considering what her husband condemned countless others to, not least the star of most of the other windows. Nonetheless, the angel puts a consoling arm around her. If this were not an image created during the buttoned-up days of the mid-19th century, one might be tempted to suggest that its purpose was to show that God's love is so great that it extends even to the whingers of the world.

There is one further piece of Victorian vandalism that cannot be ascribed to Robert Vaughan. Search carefully and you'll find, on the back of a pew, an inexpertly scratched graffito containing a set of initials and the date 11 June 1857.

But it would be regrettable to end on such a note. Rather, take a moment to climb the steps to the gallery once more and feast your eyes upon Colonel William Salusbury's temple of wonders. If nothing else, it proves that, just occasionally, good taste can be overrated. 🖾

48 LLANRHYCHWYN CHURCH
LLANRHYCHWYN

Seek out the window behind the altar, which represents an extremely early attempt at painting on glass.

SPIRITUAL ORIENTATION

The Church in Wales

PHYSICAL ORIENTATION

Llanrhychwyn, Trefriw, Conwy LL27 0YT
Grid reference: SH 774 616
OS Landranger map 115

PUBLIC TRANSPORT

The hamlet of Llanrhychwyn and the church that lies a little beyond it is about 2 miles from Llanrwst railway station, which is on the picturesque Conwy Valley Line (arrivatrainswales.co.uk; 0333 3211202). There is no bus service but the church can be reached by cycling along minor roads or via footpaths from the south side of Llanrwst's Pont Fawr.

OPENING ARRANGEMENTS

Open during daylight hours.

SERVICES

2pm 4th Sunday June to August (Evensong)
2pm 4th Sunday September (Harvest Festival)
2pm Sunday before Christmas (Carol Service).

espite being only a couple of miles away from the Conwy Valley railway line, the meagre collection of houses that makes up Llanrhychwyn ('Rhychwyn's church') seems somehow very remote. High up above the surrounding countryside and all but lost in the woods, the church is hidden away in a farmer's field behind a screen of trees. It's a curiously low-key location for a church that has gained a certain fame through its claim to be the oldest in Wales.

Rhychwyn, one of the many sons of Prince Helig ap Glannog credited with founding churches in the area, is said to have established one of wood or wattle on this site in the 6th century. The current stone building is much later though – its oldest parts date from the late 11th or early 12th century. It is known locally as 'Old Llywelyn's Church' after Llywelyn ap Iorwerth (1172–1240), who may have been responsible for later work on the church. He became Prince of Gwynedd and, in time, the de facto Prince of Wales. He had a court down in the valley where the village of Trefriw can now be found, and he and his family would hike up to this church in the hills of a Sunday.

Llanrhychwyn is a squat little thing. For a church in such an elevated spot, it's surprisingly inconspicuous. It has no proud tower or spire and even the bell-cote is masked by a stand of trees, so that you almost have to be on top of the church before you notice it's there at all. It's not even on a road – access is gained by passing through a kissing-gate and walking across the corner of a field, where a craggy dry-stone wall ends at a lychgate.

Someone has a played a trick here that has no doubt fooled many people over the years. The date on the wooden lintel of the lychgate – 1462 – is the result of some prankster having given the original second number, a 7, an extra line. The visitor passes under it into a small but ancient churchyard, many of whose slate headstones are bent low towards the earth as if burdened by the news they convey, but have otherwise borne the centuries of harsh winters surprisingly well.

The oldest parts of the church are encountered first. The entrance doorway and the fabulously thick south wall it crudely penetrates are probably late 11th century. The oak door looks magnificently old, even down to the little twig that keeps the catch in place.

Unusually, the church consists of two aisles. The one you enter contains the altar table and is the older, while the far one was added in the early 1500s, probably by Meredydd ab Ieuan. The south wall becomes noticeably thinner at the east end, a feature that strongly suggests that the chancel was added later than the 11th century, though there's some debate as to whether it occurred in the 13th or 15th.

Some ancient churches don't feel particularly old as you step into them. This is not the case with Llanrhychwyn. You have the sense of entering a damp dark cave whose possessions have not been moved for so long that they have become as one with the fabric of the church. Just inside the door, there's an ancient bier hanging on the wall that does not look as though it has seen service for many a year. The square font may indeed be even older than the church, while the beams that have held the roof up for eight centuries are the oldest of their kind in Wales. The altar rails in the south aisle and the north aisle's pulpit-cum-reading desk (with curious scratches all over it, as if carried out by a bored schoolboy) are from the two ends of the 17th century, while the bell up aloft dates from the 13th. In this context, a vernacular bench with the year 1769 inscribed on it seems like something brought in from Ikea.

At the east end of the north aisle, just by the pulpit, is a stained-glass window from 1533. Saints Mary and John stand either side of the crucified Christ, while St David and Rhychwyn feature below. Unusually for such an early piece of glasswork, the artist has made a stab at perspective in the representation of the cross. Beneath is a fragment of the Latin inscription requesting prayers for those who paid for the window to be installed.

However, the great treasure of the church is one easily overlooked. It is an even earlier window, in the south aisle behind the altar. This two-light affair dates from the 15th century and is not made of stained glass as such, since the glass itself is not coloured. Rather, it has been decorated with a brown line and a yellow stain. One scene shows the Holy Trinity while the other depicts the Madonna and Child, though the only part of Mary to have made it into the 21st century is her hands. As befits what may well be the oldest church in Wales, this may also be the nation's oldest surviving glass.

What with the church's monstrously thick walls and the lack of traffic troubling the nearby lane, a special sort of silence seems to prevail inside Llanrhychwyn, as if imported from a long ago age, when everything was just a little less frenetic. 🖾

49 ST TRILLO'S CHAPEL
RHOS-ON-SEA

It's staggering to think that the holy well, in what is Britain's smallest working church, is the same one used by St Trillo one-and-a-half millennia ago.

SPIRITUAL ORIENTATION

The Church in Wales

PHYSICAL ORIENTATION

Marine Drive, Rhos Point, Rhos-on-Sea, Conwy LL28 4PP

Grid reference: SH 841 811

OS Landranger map 116

PUBLIC TRANSPORT

From Colwyn Bay railway station (arrivatrainswales. co.uk; 0333 3211202), walk for five minutes to Kwiks on the Conway Road and take the no. 12 bus (arrivabus. co.uk) to the Cayley Arms on Rhos Promenade, from where it is a five-minute stroll along the prom. The chapel is a little beyond Rhos Point. NB There are two St Trillo's in Rhos-on-Sea – the other one is the parish church and, though worth a visit, is a very much larger building.

OPENING ARRANGEMENTS

Open daily.

SERVICES

8.30am Fridays (Eucharist)

11am 1st and 3rd Sunday (Eucharist)

10am 2nd Sunday (Matins).

Even if St Trillo's were not famous for being the smallest working church in Britain, it's easy to imagine that it might have achieved notoriety on account of its location. Walk along the promenade of the little North Welsh seaside resort of Rhos-on-Sea and you'll find it tucked away where, if it is not sacrilegious to say so, one might more readily expect a public convenience. The fact that it is about the size of a stopgap facility of that nature makes one wonder how many holidaymakers caught short on the beach have had their hopes raised and then dashed when they notice the tiny cross on the roof. Indeed, it is so small that it looks like it has been cobbled together one afternoon by a few energetic dads who got carried away trying to outdo their offsprings' sandcastles.

Unlike some churches that have physically grown and then shrunk as their fortunes have waxed and waned, Capel Sant Trillo (pronounced trith-lo) has always been very small. It's just 8ft by 11ft inside and if it weren't for its 2ft-thick walls, it would be even smaller than Bremilham (p38) – where there is merely an annual service – and be the undisputed holder of

the title of Britain's Smallest Church. The building is perhaps best described as a stone shed, though one with low and seemingly superfluous buttresses on its seaward side. Hemmed in by a high wall and partially hidden from promenaders by a line of shrubs, there is no room for a graveyard in the pocket-sized grounds.

The first building to have stood on this spot was a cell constructed by the saint himself after landing here in the 6th century. He established his little enclosure or *llan* around a well, which must have proved a very handy source of drinking water. Later, it would attract the sick and the lame from miles around who drank from it in the hope of a miraculous cure.

The altar stands directly above the well, which still supplies holy water for use at local christenings.

Trillo's cell would have been made of wattle and daub (rods interlaced with branches or twigs and smothered with clay or something similar), perhaps reinforced or protected with stones from the beach. In the saint's time, this area would have been an island of marshland bounded by two rivers, though you have to go to the west of the town to encounter any marshes today. The *llan* he created is of course long gone, and the age of the current chapel is much debated. It's possible that Cistercian monks from the nearby Rhos Fynach Abbey erected the

first stone building here, but the stone-and-mortar chapel we see today may be mostly of 16th- or 17th-century origin. Whenever it was built, by the 1890s it was in a bit of a dilapidated state and was comprehensively restored by one William Horton, though only reconsecrated in 1935 on St Trillo's Day (16 June).

Stooping through the door to pass inside, the combination of a very low whitewashed barrel-vaulted ceiling and a rough stone floor lend the place the quality of a grotto. There's just about room for half a dozen small wooden chairs (weddings held here are necessarily select affairs). A shelf doubles as an altar and is often crowded with vases of flowers. You'll sometimes find a candle burning in front of the small wooden cross and a handful of prayer requests scribbled on slips of

paper and pinned to a corkboard. It must be said that a fair amount of kitsch and oddments have found their way in too: pound-shop ceramic angels, teddy bears and porcelain books bearing saccharine couplets of the 'love/heaven above' variety battle for position with leaflets advertising the Welsh Highland Railway. On all this, St Elian and St Trillo gaze down wearily from their tiny stained-glass windows.

Only the outline of St Trillo's life has survived the whips and scorns of time. He was a member of a Celtic family from Brittany, the son of a king called Ithel Hael. An acolyte of St Cadfan, with whom he came to Wales, he ended up becoming an abbot revered for his holiness. A sister and brother of his, Llechid and Tegai, founded churches in the area as well, while he himself is believed to have established Llandrillo ('Trillo's church') over at Llandrillo yn Edeirnion in Denbighshire.

If your visit to the chapel happens to coincide with a low tide, head a little way southeast along the prom to Rhos Point. Here you should be able to make out an ancient fishing weir, though the wooden stakes that trapped the fish on the ebbing tide have been removed to spare the hulls of boats. Dating from at least 1215, the weir was in use right up until World War I. For a long period in the Middle Ages it was operated by the Rhos Fynach monks, who are said to have often repaired to the chapel to pray for a good catch. ▨

50 LLANGWYFAN

CRIBINAU

Walking out at low tide to the church perched in the middle of its own tiny island is a uniquely memorable experience.

SPIRITUAL ORIENTATION

The Church in Wales

PHYSICAL ORIENTATION

Porth Cwyfan, Llangwyfan, Tycroes, Ynys Môn LL63 5YR
Grid reference: SH 336 683
OS Landranger map 114

PUBLIC TRANSPORT

From Tycroes railway station (arrivatrainswales.co.uk; 0333 3211202), take the 25 bus (eifionscoaches.co.uk; 01407 721111) to Aberffraw. It's a pleasant 1.5-mile walk along a lane to the coast (follow signs to 'Eglwys Cwyfan') and a further 200yd along the beach. In summer, the island is accessible roughly from two hours after high tide to two hours before the next high tide. In winter, especially in rough weather, the island can become inaccessible even at low tide.

OPENING ARRANGEMENTS

The church is kept locked. Ring Rev Madalaine Brady beforehand (01407 810412) to organise a visit.

SERVICES

An afternoon service is held once a month in June, July and August. The dates and times vary each year to coincide with the low tide. Ring Rev Madalaine Brady (as above) for details.

azing down from the country lane that winds its way from the Anglesey village of Aberffraw to Porth Cwyfan, the viewer is distracted from the marvellous spectacle of the Irish Sea and its Snowdonian backdrop by what looks a most improbable sight. A very short distance from the coast lies a minute oval-shaped isle with smooth vertical sides as if a cook had run a spatula around it to tidy it up. On top, in a puddle of green, sits a little church, looking for all the world like an oversized cake decoration.

Although the church's 0.3-acre island is officially named Cribinau, locally it is known as Llangwyfan or Eglwys Cwyfan (both mean 'Cwyfan's Church'), or the mellifluous Eglwys yn y Môr Cwyfan Sant ('St Cwyfan's Church in the Sea'). It is built of sandstone grit and schist and is only accessible at low tide across a belt of rocks that have been stripped of seaweed. A set of stone steps takes the visitor up the 20ft to the church and its tiny churchyard.

The origins of Llangwyfan are obscure but the earliest stonework dates from the 12th century and it may have been built at the behest of some local lord who perhaps also donated the island for that purpose. Cribinau itself may have already had some

spiritual significance, either for the early Christians or the Pagans who came before them, since islands were places special to both groups. The Cwyfan to whom the church is dedicated is probably St Kevin, whose base at Glendalough in Ireland is a relatively short boat trip away.

The 14th and 15th centuries saw major alterations take place, most notably the slight lengthening of the nave and the subsequent building of an aisle, parallel to the existing nave, which doubled the size of the church. An arcade of three arches gave access from one to the other, and when the aisle collapsed or was otherwise demolished in the first half of the 19th

century, these arches were bricked up. Their outlines can still be clearly made out along the northwest wall.

However, the church's location had proved problematic long before the demise of the aisle. Notwithstanding the loss of parts of the churchyard into the sea as the island eroded, storms and high tides often made the causeway impassable. For many years a room in the mansion house of Llangwyfan Isaf was used as a stand-by on such occasions, the rector leading the service being entitled to a breakfast of two eggs and a cup of small beer to compensate him for making the trip, which wasn't a bad deal given that it's

only half a mile away. Eventually, in 1870, a new parish church was built on the mainland, and a couple of decades later Llangwyfan was a ruin. Various fundraising efforts since then have helped to restore the church to its current state.

The interior is very humble. Within whitewashed walls, a few rows of chairs face a pulpit and a small wooden table adorned with a simple cross and two candlesticks. The most noticeable feature is the row of filled-in arches that are all that is left of the doomed northwest aisle.

It's hard to believe that this church was once at the centre of a mighty battle, not so much between the Welsh and the

English as between Welsh and English. In 1766, the Bishop of Bangor sent an elderly English priest, Dr Thomas Bowles, to serve Llangwyfan. Like most English people, then as now, he spoke no Welsh at all, while of the 500-odd parishioners of Trefdraeth only five spoke English.

Understandably miffed at having their church services made incomprehensible, the parishioners took their case to the Court of Arches (an ecclesiastical court that still exists today), requesting that a Welsh-speaking priest be appointed in place of Dr Bowles. The court was not one of the most expeditious arbitrators ever known. It received evidence in May 1770

but it wasn't until January 1773 that a ruling was handed down.

The parishioners asserted that Bowles' lack of Welsh contravened three different laws including the Act for the Translation of the Scriptures into Welsh (1563). The Bishop of Bangor's lawyers countered that the parishioners must prove that Bowles could not utter a single word of Welsh.

The judgment was a classic legal fudge. George Hay, the judge presiding over the court, ruled that Welsh-speaking parishes could only be served by Welsh-speaking clergy, but, since Bowles was already serving there, he could not be removed. Thankfully for all concerned,

the doctor had the good grace to die 10 months later. The next vicar of Llangwyfan was Richard Griffith, a Welsh speaker.

A rather kinder, though probably apocryphal, story has attached itself to the church and its tiny island. One night, the locals are said to have saved a ship from wrecking itself on the rocky coastline by lighting fires that alerted its captain to the danger he was in. Some time later the grateful skipper asked them if he could do anything to repay their kind deed. They told him that the island was crumbling and that it was putting their church at risk. He duly took the building of the wall in hand and the church, like his ship, was saved. 🦋

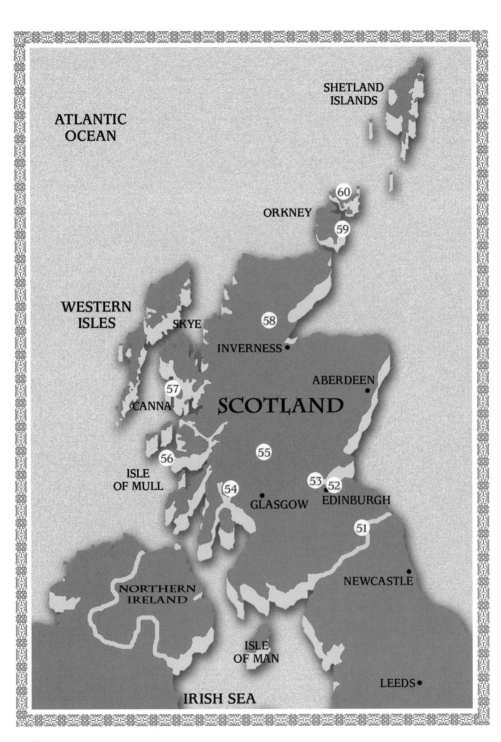

ATLANTIC
OCEAN

SHETLAND
ISLANDS

60

ORKNEY

59

WESTERN
ISLES

SKYE

58

INVERNESS

ABERDEEN

57

CANNA

SCOTLAND

56

ISLE
OF MULL

55

54

53 52

GLASGOW

EDINBURGH

51

NORTHERN
IRELAND

NEWCASTLE

ISLE
OF MAN

LEEDS

IRISH SEA

SCOTLAND

51 HOSELAW CHAPEL
HOSELAW

The highlight is the wonderful surprise of finding a delicately frescoed apse in an otherwise unsophisticated building.

SPIRITUAL ORIENTATION
Church of Scotland

PHYSICAL ORIENTATION
Hoselaw, Borders TD5 8BP
Grid reference: NT 801 317
OS Landranger map 74

PUBLIC TRANSPORT
Hoselaw Chapel finds itself in a bit of a public transport vacuum. If coming from Edinburgh, probably your best bet is to take the 52 bus (perrymansbuses.co.uk;

01289 308719) to the attractive abbey town of Kelso and get a taxi the last 6 miles from there.

OPENING ARRANGEMENTS
Open during daylight hours.

SERVICES
Occasional evening Communion services and a Good Friday vigil are held. For further information contact the Cheviot Churches' session clerk: linda.afleming@btinternet.com.

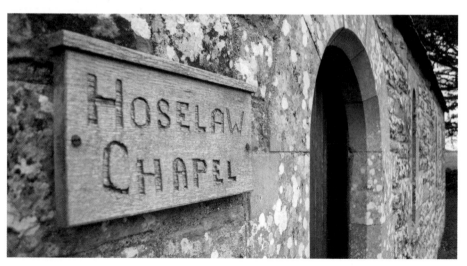

nclosed by a dry-stone wall in various states of repair, Hoselaw Chapel stands perilously close to the border with England. Beyond Hoselaw Loch, immediately to the east, the Cheviot Hills mark the frontier with their customary desolate beauty. There's an undeniably austere feel to Hoselaw Chapel too. Dropped as if by chance at the side of a road that has little but farmland for company, the tiny kirk is a drip of sombre grey paint on an otherwise cheerful green canvas. Even the line of protective trees that stands behind it struggles to soften its severe demeanour. The building appears to do nothing to beguile into stopping and lingering awhile the meagre trickle of travellers who find themselves on this back road. Things are not quite as they seem though, for on closer inspection there is something that hints of possible treasures within. At the eastern end of the nave, all but hidden by foliage, is the

surprising sight of a trim little apse topped by a domed roof.

Stepping through the plain round-arched doorway, it is the interior's walls that catch the eye. While the white freestone of which they are built has weathered grey on the outside (and even a dull red around the apse), within they are an appealing light cream colour, speckled with the occasional stone of a lime green or orange hue.

Around 50 chairs in neat rows all but fill the nave below a ruddy-brown wooden roof. The only other furnishings are a simple lectern and an attractive stone font that appears to have been made specially for the chapel. This is not found near the door as one would expect but has been placed at the front, on the left-hand side, presumably as a visual counterweight to the lectern to the right. Its circular bowl, supported by a base nearly as wide as itself, is engraved with a pattern of wavy lines suggestive of water. It bears the words 'Except a man be born of water and of the Spirit he cannot enter the Kingdom of God', and is capped by a wooden lid to which an intricate brass plate has been attached. Immediately behind it, a doorway leads off into a small vestry.

But it is what lies beyond the Normanesque Byzantine arch that rewards the visitor to this chapel. Painted on the domed ceiling are three golden-haired angels carrying a scroll that reads 'Alleluia for the Lord God Omnipotent Reigneth'. To be honest, both the painting and the ceiling could do with some love and attention but the angels' coral wings and pastel blue smocks are a delight.

Below them, the apse's solitary window is a peculiarly small affair that barely lights the carved wooden altar. It shows Jesus holding a golden grail and dressed in the sort of princely robes that he would doubtless have eschewed in his earthly life.

Two plaques on the wall tell the brief history of the chapel. One is dedicated to Dr Thomas Leishman, in whose memory the chapel was built in 1906 as a mark of the esteem in which he was held by the local populace. The son of a clergyman, Leishman became a theologian and writer, and was minister to the local parish from 1855 to 1895. In 1892 he co-founded the Scottish Church Society, a body within the Church of Scotland that still exists today.

Despite spending almost all of his entire working life in the ecclesiastical backwater that is the parish of Linton, he was invited to become Moderator of the General Assembly of the Church of

Scotland in 1898, just six years before his death.

The other plaque is devoted to his third son, James Fleming Leishman, who succeeded him as minister at Linton. Just as his father had done, Leishman junior served the parish for exactly 40 years.

A much earlier place of worship, first documented in 1421, once stood very close by. It was attached to Kelso Abbey and dedicated to St Machute, a 6th-century missionary. The chapel must have been quickly abandoned because by 1560 it was already reported as being a ruin. It may though have had one brush with history in its short life. Today, visitors can walk right round the narrow grassy strip that encircles the church without encountering a single gravestone.

However, there was apparently a graveyard here during the time of the first chapel. In 1513, James IV of Scotland suffered a disastrous defeat at Flodden, just over the border, near the Northumbrian village of Branxton. The king and most of the Scots nobles present were killed and tradition has it that the bodies of those who died alongside them were transported back to be buried in good Scottish soil here at Hoselaw. It should be said, though, that exactly the same story is told of the churchyard at Kirk Yetholm, so perhaps not too much store should be set by the tale.

52 ST MARGARET'S CHAPEL
EDINBURGH CASTLE

The experience of entering the oldest building in Edinburgh, barely changed since St David himself constructed it, is one to be savoured.

SPIRITUAL ORIENTATION

Non-denominational (Historic Environment Scotland)

PHYSICAL ORIENTATION

Edinburgh Castle, Castlehill, Edinburgh EH1 2NG
Grid reference: NT 251 734
OS Landranger map 66

PUBLIC TRANSPORT

Edinburgh Castle is in the heart of the Scottish capital, at the top of the Royal Mile, a few minutes' walk from Edinburgh Waverley station (scotrail.co.uk; 0344 8110141). Once inside, St Margaret's Chapel is well signposted, and is beside the huge gun known as Mons Meg.

OPENING ARRANGEMENTS

Open daily whenever Edinburgh Castle is open (entry fee to the castle). Further details: edinburghcastle.gov.uk; 0131 225 9846.

SERVICES

The St Margaret's Chapel Guild holds an annual service on St Margaret's Day (16 November). Further details: stmargaretschapel.com.

isit Edinburgh Castle and you will spy an exposed and anonymous box of dark stone apparently attempting to defend itself by means of an outsize gun from whatever the North Wind may throw at it. It puts you in mind of those Arabian soldiers of old who tried to see off Saharan sandstorms by charging them on horseback, slashing at the wind with their scimitars. Even on approaching the box it does not look any more chapel-like (though the medieval siege bombard – Mons Meg – is clearly a weapon). It is only on closer inspection that you notice that the small round-arched windows are filled with stained glass and that the doorway is ever so slightly fancy.

It is strange to think that this unprepossessing structure is not only the oldest part of Edinburgh Castle but also the oldest complete building in the Scottish capital. Perhaps unsurprisingly it is the most venerable surviving church in Scotland as well as its smallest. It was built around 1130 and measures just 16ft 6in by 10ft 6in.

The woman to whom the chapel is dedicated is surely one of the best-connected saints of all time. Margaret was

a granddaughter of Edmund Ironside, who was King of England for seven months in 1016. She was born in the village of Mecseknadas in Hungary but came to England as a child in 1057. She would have preferred the life of the cloister but, at the age of 20, she was badgered into marrying King Malcolm III of Scotland, 20 years her senior. His father was the Duncan who was so famously murdered by Macbeth. Margaret had two daughters and six sons with Malcolm. Her three younger boys all became King of Scotland (the youngest, David, also going on to sainthood), while both a daughter and granddaughter became Queen of England, all of which many may see as a very good argument for republicanism.

She was also a woman given to holiness, humility and service to the poor, attributes she encouraged in her subjects by forcing reforms upon them and founding numerous churches and chapels. This particular chapel, however, was probably erected by her son David, though it may have incorporated the oratory that Margaret is said to have established on the very highest point of this extinct volcano.

A further restoration and refurbishment occurred in 1993.

Passing inside, its past as a store for high explosives is less easily put out of mind – the bomb-proof vaulting installed as a safety measure remains in place, giving the chapel the feel of a tunnel, albeit a very short one. Three of the outer walls are 2ft thick, meaning that the space inside is very small indeed – just about enough for 20 people if they hold conservative views on elbow use.

This all-round insulation has the effect of cutting out nearly all the noise of Scotland's second-most popular tourist attraction. Suddenly, the patter and clatter of feet on cobbles and the squeals of excitable schoolchildren are silenced and visitors are pleasantly becalmed. This is a place that says, 'The devil take your stereo and your record collection: here we shall have silence, and when that silence is to be broken, we shall sing the old songs.'

The most eye-catching feature is the original chancel arch, decorated with the familiar chevron mouldings. Beyond is an apse, which comes as a surprise because the outside of the eastern wall is flat rather than semicircular. The altar is draped with the St Margaret altar cloth, whose many signs, symbols and colours are explained in a booklet sold in the castle.

One rather lovely oddity concerns the flower arrangements with which the chapel is beautified each week. These are

Though outwardly far from comely and often poorly maintained, the chapel clearly held a soft spot in the hearts of the Scottish people. In 1329, no less a man than King Robert the Bruce spoke of St Margaret's while on his deathbed. One of his final actions was to give orders that repairs be made to it.

It is not entirely David's fault that the chapel looks so uninspiring from the outside because after the Reformation it was adapted for service as a gunpowder store. Before long, its original purpose had been completely forgotten and it wasn't until 1845, when the antiquary Sir Daniel Wilson recognised the building for what it was, that it became a place of worship again. However, renovation of the building did not take place until the late 1920s.

produced by the St Margaret's Chapel Guild, which was formed in 1942. Echoing the Red-Headed League of the Sherlock Holmes adventures, to become a member of the guild, you have to be called Margaret. The very first Margaret to provide flowers was the guild's then patron, the princess of that name. The guild was also responsible for the installation of the modern oak artefacts inside the chapel: the bench seats, an alms chest and table, a flower stand and the display case that holds the St Margaret's Gospel Book. All were crafted into being by the renowned cabinetmaker Piers Kettlewell.

However, the most successful of the 20th-century incursions are arguably the five small stained-glass windows made in 1922 by Douglas Strachan. He was perhaps the pre-eminent stained-glass window artist of his time and his work can also be seen at the castle's Scottish National War Memorial, as well as at another tiny church, St Mary of the Angels (p134) in Brownshill, Gloucestershire. Four of his windows here depict saints: Margaret, Ninian, Andrew and Columba respectively. The fifth portrays William Wallace. It would no doubt tickle the old campaigner to find himself in such righteous company.

ST PETER'S
LINLITHGOW

The highlight here is a literal one, in that the semi-glazed dome in the roof is not only eye-catching but also allows the sun to illuminate the church.

SPIRITUAL ORIENTATION
Scottish Episcopal Church

PHYSICAL ORIENTATION
153 High Street, Linlithgow, West Lothian EH49 7EJ
Grid reference: NT 000 770
OS Landranger map 65

PUBLIC TRANSPORT
The church can be found near the heart of Linlithgow, and just 0.3 miles west of the town's railway station (scotrail.co.uk; 0344 8110141), between the steeply rising streets of Lion Well Wynd and Dog Well Wynd.

OPENING ARRANGEMENTS
Contact Rev Christine Barclay (01506 846069) to arrange a visit.

SERVICES
Sunday 9.30am (Sung Eucharist)
Tuesday 10.30am (Said Eucharist)
Further details at stpeterslinlithgow.co.uk.

I f you were asked what building you might find wedged between a chip shop and a hairdressers on the high street of the lively little town of Linlithgow, it might be some while before you hazarded a guess at it being a Byzantine-style church. Even more bafflingly, St Peter's is not a place of worship thrown up by a community of homesick Eastern Orthodox refugees but the home of a local congregation of Scots folk who, prior to its construction, had led a peripatetic existence that rivalled the 40 years Moses and his fellow Israelites spent wandering about the desert.

It wasn't until the start of the 20th century that Episcopalians in Scotland came out from under the shadow of the persecution they had long suffered. In 1912, local members of the denomination organised themselves into a body called St Peter's Episcopal Mission in Linlithgow. With no building of their own, they met for worship in a bewildering array of locations, including the Court Room of the Burgh Halls, various shops, a defunct pub, a hall on the High Street (requisitioned by the army in 1914), the vacant Craigmailen United Free Church (forced out by dry rot), and some apparently highly disagreeable premises belonging to the Scotch Girls Friendly Society.

It was only in 1924 when the congregation's priest-in-charge, Rev W S

Snow, alerted the Bishop of Edinburgh to their plight that building plans took shape in earnest. The good bishop, George Henry Somerset Walpole, put down £100 to secure a site on the High Street on which a church could be erected, and promised a further £500 from the proceeds of a lecture tour he was about to give in the United States.

The excited congregation, numbering about 80 (and now uprooted once again to a room at the Palace Hotel), had plans

drawn up by architect J Walker Todd. It must have been one of the stranger briefs of his career, for the church had to slide in between two buildings not much more than 26ft apart. Necessity proved the mother of invention and gave Scotland one of her more unusual churches.

Todd's solution to the problem of getting light into a building in such a confined space was to borrow from the churches of Byzantium, whose domed roofs capture the sun's rays to illuminate the congregation within. He estimated that his design would cost about £1,600 to build, a sum approaching £700,000 in today's money. On noting that their kitty, after many years of fundraising, amounted to a mere £6, the Episcopalians trimmed their cloth and asked him for a less ambitious set of plans. He obliged and the cost was cut to a slightly more manageable £1,000.

The foundation stone was laid by Colonel Maclaren of the Craigs on 18 May 1927 and the Byzantine-style church was completed almost exactly a year later. It was consecrated on 30 May 1928 by Bishop Walpole, just 475 years after the final collapse of the empire whose architecture it celebrated.

Rather than calling the new church St Peter's, as one might have expected, Bishop Walpole contrived to dedicate the church to St Mildred, the saint with whom his late wife had shared a name. The church was lumbered with this moniker for the next 50 years (and its unfortunate nickname, St Mildew's), by which time it was decided that the bishop's wife had been sufficiently honoured and St Mildred gave way to St Peter.

However, fans of the patron saint of the Isle of Thanet will be pleased to learn that she has not been expunged from the church altogether. She appears in one of the three small, elevated and well-executed coloured-glass windows behind the altar – the only windows in the church aside from those found high up in the domed roof. Perhaps in order not to make her seem too holy to relate to, the artist who created the window – a 'Miss Howson, daughter of the Archdeacon of Warrington' – has seen fit to give her a rather fetching pair of purple slippers. The left-hand window depicts Margaret, the mother of St David (see St Margaret's Chapel, Edinburgh Castle, p267). Between these two women is a crucified Christ.

The church itself is laid out in the form of a Greek cross. Its dimensions (c.40ft long, 25ft wide and 30ft high) put you in mind of one of those old blue police boxes and, true to form, it does seem oddly larger on the inside than it appears on the outside. The limitations imposed upon the architect by the church's location mean that the nave lies north–south, with the altar contained in an apse at the

southern end rather than to the east, as might be expected.

The features that most visibly lend the church its Byzantine feel are the 'sunbursts' of painted slate above the internal archways, and the fish-scale pattern in the window on the north wall, which is repeated in the eight windows of the circular dome in the roof. The splendid symmetry of the dome is best seen from a supine position in the middle of the church floor, though you may wish to warn other visitors of your intentions before attempting the same.

To the rear of the church is a small garden in what remains of the 'toft' of land attached to the property. The three antique wooden benches there once graced the platforms of Linlithgow railway station. They offer a good vantage point from which to view the apse and dome of this tiny piece of old Byzantium near the shore of Linlithgow Loch.

COLINTRAIVE CHURCH
COLINTRAIVE

Notice this church's unusual glass doors that allow a view of the Kyles of Bute and the boats sailing up and down it.

SPIRITUAL ORIENTATION
Church of Scotland

PHYSICAL ORIENTATION
Kyles View, Colintraive,
Argyll & Bute PA22 3AS
Grid reference: NS 044 734
OS Landranger map 63

PUBLIC TRANSPORT
Colintraive Church is actually about 1.5 miles southeast of the village of Colintraive, along the coast road. Although there is a school bus between the two, you'll almost certainly end up walking the distance if you arrive by public transport. Colintraive itself has a relatively good bus service, despite being a small village. If you can get yourself to either Dunoon or Rothesay (both have good links with Glasgow by ferry and bus), you can take the 479 bus (westcoastmotors.co.uk; 01586 552319) from either to Colintraive and walk down the coast.

OPENING ARRANGEMENTS
Open daily.

SERVICES
10.45am 1st and 2nd Sunday.

raw a line 30 miles northwest from Glasgow and you'll come to an area of Argyll that is slowly disintegrating, split into peninsula after peninsula by the deep scissor-cuts of sea lochs. Make your way onto one of these islands-in-waiting – bounded by lochs Riddon and Striven – and on its southwestern shore you'll come to the trimmest little stone-built chapel of ease you could wish for. Today it continues to serve the surrounding community and stands as a memorial to a remarkable young woman.

A mile south of the village after which it takes its name, Colintraive Church offers to the world a clean white western façade and a bright blue door. Its roof is topped with something of an aspirational bell-cote complete with a finial so tall it almost amounts to a spire.

The driving force behind the building of the church was Janet Campbell, a woman who concerned herself with the spiritual needs of the workers and tenants on her husband John's estate and of other inhabitants dotted about the district. Their parish was a large one and, until the opening of Colintraive Church in 1840, each Sunday they faced a long walk over to the other side of the peninsula followed by a boat trip across Loch Striven to the

parish church at Inverchaolain. In such circumstances, it cannot have been pleasant to hear the heavens open as the sermon was drawing to a close.

For the first 70 years of its life Colintraive flitted between denominations, blown about by the prevailing winds of Scottish ecclesiastical politics. Just three years after it was opened it left the Church of Scotland for the Free Church of Scotland. This was a result of the so-called Disruption, when a rancorous dispute over what many saw as the overbearing role of the gentry in church affairs saw more than a third of congregations jumping ship to form their own denomination. In 1900 Colintraive joined the United Free Church of Scotland (an affiliation of the Free Church of Scotland and the United Presbyterian Church of Scotland). Things came full circle in 1929 when the United Free Church of Scotland returned to the fold and merged with the Church of Scotland. No doubt fatigued by its wanderings and wary that its next move might be a Pythonesque desertion to the Judean Popular People's Front, it has remained with the official state church ever since.

Aside from the pleasing oddity that is the bell-cote finial, Colintraive is so simple it resembles a child's drawing of a church.

Set in a compact graveyard, it comprises a nave with a small vestry hidden away at its eastern end. Two lancet windows flank the front door, which has been given an arch just a little too plain to be termed a flourish but which is at least in the same attractive light stone as the bell-cote. Each side wall has been fitted with three arched windows, all of the same size and placed at regular intervals.

Inside, the church is awash with purple, burnt umber and little splashes of pink. These are the respective colours of the hymnal, Bible and children's song books that fill the ledges at the front of every box pew. Since the box pews themselves all but fill the church, the overall effect is of an art installation created by a latter-day disciple of Mondrian, and is all the more charming for being unconsciously done.

Two rather more deliberate artworks are the stained-glass windows at the west end of the church, donated by the McFeat family. One depicts a behaloed crusader and is dedicated to their son Matthew, who was killed in World War I; while the other is in memory of all the fallen of Colintraive during that conflict. Between them is a modern glass door that must be a great distraction for preachers because it means that if the outer door is open, they have a delightful view of the Isle of Bute. The church is doubtless a handy landmark for sailors as they slide up and down the Kyles of Bute, the strip of water that separates the mainland from the island.

Look above the door to the church and you'll see the marble memorial to Janet Campbell, whose austerity of design is offset by a heart-felt inscription. The daughter of a renowned Glaswegian entrepreneur called Kirkman Finlay, Campbell married the laird of South Hall, near Colintraive. She initially threw herself into the task of running a 'Sabbath School' for the local children but in 1837 set herself the challenge of raising the estimated £400 that it would cost to establish a church on a patch of estate land on the western shore beneath Beinn Bhreac.

As it turned out, the final bill was somewhat above that mark, but the shortfall was made up by her husband. The very first service was conducted by Rev Alexander MacTavish on 23 August 1840 but, sadly, Janet and John Campbell were unable to attend. They had travelled south in an attempt to restore Janet to health, a vain quest as it turned out, for she died seven weeks after the opening of the church.

The couple's grand home has since been demolished and the Campbell name has disappeared from South Hall, but Janet would no doubt be content that this church is her lasting legacy here. 🏵

ST FILLAN'S
KILLIN

This white-walled, teal-roofed church is one of the finest and oldest tin tabernacles you'll ever have the pleasure of seeing.

SPIRITUAL ORIENTATION

Scottish Episcopal Church/ Roman Catholic

PHYSICAL ORIENTATION

Main Street, Killin, Stirlingshire FK21 8UW
Grid reference: NN 573 331
OS Landranger map 51

PUBLIC TRANSPORT

The village of Killin has not had a railway station since 1965 (the closest is at Crianlarich, 14 miles away) but is served by several buses, including the 913 between Edinburgh and Fort William; the 973 between Dundee and Oban; and the 978 between Edinburgh and Oban (all citylink.co.uk; 0141 3329644). All routes pass through Crianlarich. The church is towards the northern end of the village at the junction of Main Street and Station Road.

OPENING ARRANGEMENTS

Contact church secretary Gina Angus (01567 820238) to arrange a visit. If she is away, someone from a shop called the Outdoor Centre opposite the church may be able to let you in.

SERVICES

9.45am Sunday in summer; 11.15am in winter (Scottish Episcopal Service)
2.30pm Sunday all year (Roman Catholic Mass)
Further information: strathearnchurches.org.uk.

h, the 'tin tabernacles' – can there be anything quite as deliciously Victorian and homespun as these ugly ducklings of ecclesiastical architecture? Harbingers of the mass-produced, pre-fabricated and flat-packed world we inhabit today, they were once viewed as a godsend by vicars in rapidly expanding industrial areas whose churches were full to bursting, and by non-conformists in need of cheap premises outside the control of the state. Only around 60 of the myriad tin tabernacles erected in Scotland in the 19th and early 20th centuries have made it into

the 21st. Built in 1876 by the 7th Earl of Breadalbane as a chapel of ease for his shooting parties (spawning its nickname 'The Grouse Chapel'), St Fillan's can lay claim not only to being one of Scotland's most beautifully preserved examples but also to being the oldest of the survivors.

In late spring bumblebees busily harvest pollen from the ornamental cherries that guard the front gate. Beyond, the white walls of the church are topped by a gabled roof of teal and a bell-cote apparently lifted straight from Toy Town. As it happens, the bell-cote turns out to be a clever fake – it's actually a ventilator.

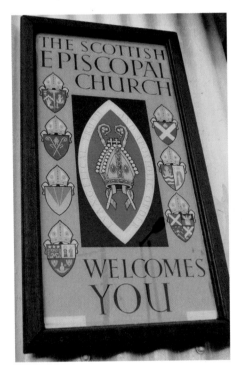

The cheap-and-cheerful and almost exclusively metallic exterior of the church does not prepare you for what is inside. Pine-clad walls give the place a Scandinavian air, while the surprising number of short wooden pews crammed into the nave make it seem larger than it is. The altar is also made of wood, by one George Watson of Edinburgh, and is not only carved but painted. The ornate altar rail before it is from the demolished chapel at Taymouth Castle in Kenmore. The scene is completed by a circular stained-glass window above the altar – the only stained glass in the church – which shows an

angel giving Mary the doubtless unexpected news that she is pregnant.

There is little decoration on the walls besides a few brass plaques. One of these rather movingly commemorates a Willie Don, who, from difficult beginnings, made it out to southern Nigeria as a curator in the Agricultural Department before dying aged 32. The memorial was placed there 'by his former companions in affectionate remembrance of the years spent together in the Boys' Home, Kenmore'.

Though the church may look all of a piece, the St Fillan's we see today was constructed in three stages. The building thrown up by the 7th Earl consisted of three bays with a porch at the western end – little more than a glorified shed. It was probably purchased from The London Iron Church & Chapel Co., of which the earl was a shareholder. It was one of four major manufacturers offering off-the-peg churches which were delivered by train and erected on the client's land around a timber frame.

Nine years later, the church was extended east and a transept added so that its floor plan formed a traditional cross shape. It remained like this until 1969 when a meeting room was appended at the eastern end beyond the chancel. Despite the enlargements, the tabernacle remains pleasingly small.

Flat-pack corrugated-iron buildings were a popular export to the colonies of the British Empire from the 1840s onwards. These lightweight, cheap and easily assembled 'wriggly tin' structures also proved attractive to those in the remoter parts of Britain. Walk around the village of Killin and you'll spot a number of corrugated-iron pre-fabs still serving as cottages and commercial premises. What makes St Fillan's so unusual is that the vast majority of tin tabernacles in Scotland belong to dissenting denominations rather than the state church. Furthermore, in a refreshing show of ecumenism, not only are Episcopal services held here but weekly Roman Catholic Masses too.

Fittingly, given the origins of this particular architectural style, the early years of St Fillan's (when it may have been known as St Peter's) had a somewhat colonial edge to them. The church was only open during the summer months, when the earl's shooting parties were tramping the country blasting away at poor benighted wildlife, and the services were then habitually taken by holidaying English clergymen.

The tabernacle was mothballed at the beginning of World War II and did not open its doors for regular worship until 1948. Ten years later, the 9th Earl gave the church into the care of the trustees of the diocese. He also donated a small plot of land next to it, which permitted the eventual building of the meeting room. The corrugated-iron sheets for this extension are reputed to have been salvaged from Tyndrum railway station. The church underwent a thorough renovation in 2011, which accounts for the seemingly pristine state in which visitors find it today.

The 8th-century Irish saint to whom the church is dedicated was the son of St Kentigerna and grandson of a prince of Leinster. He sailed to Scotland along with his mother, three brothers and uncle, St Congan, and they established themselves on the Isle of Skye. His missionary wanderings took him to many parts of the country, including Islay, Perthshire and Fife, before he made his home in Killin. You can't help feeling that he would be rather taken by the church that bears his name in his adopted village, given that it too arrived here at the end of a long journey. 🏴

THE MICHAEL CHAPEL
IONA

With its row of tall candles and chairs facing one another across the nave, this tiny chapel has an unmistakeable monastic feel.

SPIRITUAL ORIENTATION

Ecumenical (Historic Environment Scotland)

PHYSICAL ORIENTATION

Iona, Inner Hebrides, Argyll & Bute PA76 6SJ
Grid reference: NM 287 245
OS Landranger map 48

PUBLIC TRANSPORT

Unless you happen to be living on the Isle of Mull, a visit to Iona can take on the nature of a pilgrimage. From Oban railway station (scotrail.co.uk; 0344 8110141) on the west coast of Scotland, you can take a Caledonian MacBrayne ferry to Craignure on the Isle of Mull (calmac.co.uk; 0800 0665000). A bus service runs from Craignure to Fionnphort (westcoasttours. co.uk; 01631 566809) and is usually timed to connect with the ferries at both ends. From Fionnphort, it's a 10-minute crossing over the Sound of Mull to Iona (Caledonian MacBrayne again). The chapel is beside Iona Abbey.

Alternatively, there are several companies running boat tours from Oban that stop for varying lengths of time on Iona en route to various other islands. Details of these can be obtained from the Oban tourist information centre (oban. org.uk; 01631 563122).

OPENING ARRANGEMENTS

Always open. From 9.30am to 5pm an admission fee is charged. At all other times entrance is free.

SERVICES

The Iona Community leads services from November to Easter, excluding Christmas week (at all other times of year, services are held in the Abbey Church)
9.30am Monday to Saturday (Morning Collect)
7.30pm Tuesday (Healing)
7.30pm Thursday (Communion)
7.30pm Sunday (Quiet)
Further information: iona.org.uk
Occasional Catholic Masses are held throughout the year.

Iona, an insignificant shard of land on a coast liberally scattered with islands, is surely an inspiration to us all. Despite its size and location – off a remote corner of the Isle of Mull – it managed to become the cradle of Christianity in Scotland and Northumbria. Here it was that St Columba and 12 companions landed in 563, having sailed from Ireland in a flimsy coracle. Their voyage was not altogether voluntary. They had been forced into exile from

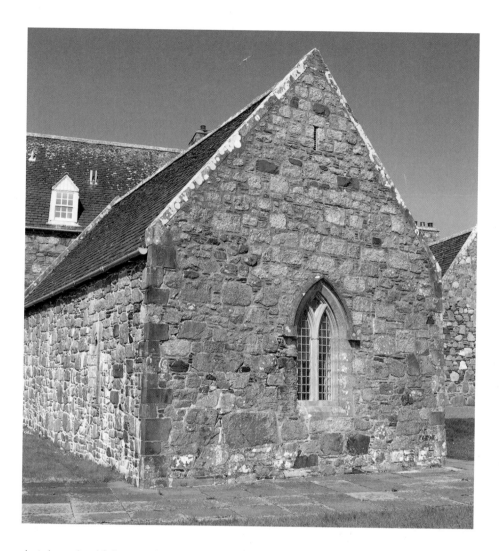

their homeland following the Battle of Cul Dreimhne. This was an extraordinary episode in which a dispute between St Columba and St Finnian over the copyright of a psalter is said to have escalated into an engagement that resulted in an estimated 3,000 casualties.

Making the best of the situation, Columba and his confederates set up a monastery on Iona and used it as a base as they travelled through Scotland and northern England preaching the gospel and founding further religious houses. Iona's monastery flourished until 794, when the first of a series of Viking raids on the island occurred, including a disastrous sacking in 802. The monks eventually threw in the towel, abandoning Iona in 849.

It wasn't until very early in the 13th century that the monastic tradition returned to the isle. A new monastery was founded by a party of Benedictines, invited over by Ranald (sometimes known as Reginald), son of Somerled, the so-called 'King of the Isles'. At the same time, Ranald asked Augustinian nuns to establish a convent on the island, his sister Bethóc becoming the first prioress.

It's a very short walk from the jetty on Iona to the monastic complex the Benedictines built. However, there is little evidence of the monastery founded by

Columba – the first church was built of wood and has left nothing but a few marks in the ground for us to remember it by – or indeed of the later churches that were established here prior to the coming of the 13th-century monks and nuns.

If it had not been for these good people's construction of the Abbey Church, the Michael Chapel would never have come into being. The monks quickly decided to build their abbey on the site of the ruined church left over from the previous monastery. However, they knew that dismantling the old church and constructing their grand new building would take time and they wanted to establish themselves as quickly as possible. Their solution was to erect a small chapel to the side of the derelict church and make use of it until such time as they could move their services into the abbey.

Today, that stopgap place of worship, now known as the Michael Chapel, is much as it looked to the monks who built it, at least externally. Only the windows, which are 16th century, would be unfamiliar to them. The chapel, which sits in the shadow of the much larger abbey behind it, consists of a simple stone-built nave with a gabled roof. The need for speed when constructing it is quite apparent, because the only original ornamentation is to be found in the doorway. This is of Norman design and runs to two arches and a hood supported by pillars, though even here you can sense the voice of the brothers urging each other to get on with it, for there is none of the intricate detailing in the arches that was the fashion at the time.

The interior of the church – which is a little piece of Africa come to the Inner Hebrides – can best be explained by returning to the history of the island. The abbey re-established Iona as an important pilgrimage destination and the Benedictine monks and Augustinian nuns continued worshipping here right up until the Reformation in 1560. The island briefly recaptured its prominence when King Charles I forced bishops on the Scottish Church and Iona became the seat of the Bishop of the Isles. After the bishops were once again expunged from the Church, the abbey lay dormant until the early 20th century when the Iona Cathedral Trust began a programme of restoration. In 1938 an ecumenical movement called the Iona Community took over the reins and in 1959 it was they who renovated the Michael Chapel, which had become quite decrepit.

In a refreshing reversal of the usual missionary pattern, much of the money for the repairs came from Africa, as did all the chapel's furniture and the wood for the wonderful barrel ceiling. The space is dominated by a long table that splits the chapel lengthways. On either side are

chairs backed by stalls that line the walls. A cross stands on a plain altar at the eastern end, and a bust of Columba decorates a window sill. The whole is dramatically lit by the eastern window and, when evening draws on, by a line of candles held high on candlesticks ranged around the church.

On your tour around Iona's other fine buildings, make sure you visit St Oran's Chapel. Of a similar shape and proportions to the Michael Chapel, it is the most venerable complete building on the island, pre-dating the coming of the Benedictines. It can be found in Reilig Òdhrain, believed to be the oldest graveyard in Scotland.

CANNA RHU CHURCH
CANNA

The Inner Hebrides are blessed with some exquisite settings and this church finds itself in one of the comeliest you could imagine.

SPIRITUAL ORIENTATION
Church of Scotland

PHYSICAL ORIENTATION
Canna, Small Isles, Inner Hebrides, Highland
PH44 4RS
Grid reference: NG 276 053
OS Landranger map 39

PUBLIC TRANSPORT
Take a train to Mallaig (scotrail.co.uk; 01752 675670) on the west coast of Scotland. Board a ferry to Canna (once daily, twice on Saturday in summer – check timetables for winter sailings: calmac.co.uk; 0800 0665000). The church is about 300yd along the one track that heads away from the pier.

OPENING ARRANGEMENTS
Open daily.

SERVICES
None.

he Isle of Canna (Canaigh in Gaelic) in the Inner Hebrides is something of a collector's item as far as ecclesiastical gatherings are concerned. The westernmost of the Small Isles may not extend to much more than four square miles and may only boast a modern-day population of 19 but in its time it has hosted both a nunnery and a monastery. The small nunnery was called Sgorr nam Bàn-naomha ('The Cliff of the Holy Women') and was established in the southwest of the island, while, to the east, the monastery – said to have been dedicated to St Columba – flourished from the 7th to the 9th century. A township called A' Chill grew up around the latter and existed until the first half of the 19th century when the island became yet another victim of the Clearances, large numbers of its tenants being forced off the land and replaced by sheep. A rather wonderful carved stone cross, a pillory post (into which miscreants had their thumbs jammed) and a burial ground bear witness to the centuries of activity here.

Canna Rhu Church (sometimes referred to as Canna Church or St Columba's Presbyterian Church) represents a relatively recent chapter in the religious history of the island – work was begun on it in 1912 and completed two years later. Designed by P MacGregor Chalmers in the pointed Gothic style, it is constructed of locally quarried rubble of surprisingly varied colours. Diverse shades of dark grey and red compete for dominance with rocks of beige and ochre hues. The thin circular bell tower at the western end resembles some sort of ballistic missile pointing into the sky and has led to the building being given the nickname 'The Rocket Church'. Three unevenly spaced lancet windows puncture the north and south walls, with another two in the eastern and western ends,

along with a tiny slit made in the tower. The building is of such a simple and rustic design that, if it were not for the smooth rendered stone roof, it would give the appearance of a chapel that has seen aeons come and go.

The church was the brainchild of Canna resident Mary Johannan Cameron (known as Johanna). She and her husband Allan Thom were keen that:

a suitable place of worship be built to serve the members of this neighbourhood and, as far as possible, to maintain religion; and church-going habits – above all to keep alive the sense of the presence of God among old and young

as a contemporary newspaper report put it. Before it was opened, Canna's Church of Scotland adherents were obliged to undertake a 30-mile voyage to the parish church. The building also stands as a memorial to Allan's father, Robert, who built the island's first pier and whose widow and daughters put up half the money for the project.

Fans of the finer points of church orientation (the word itself is derived from the positioning of a building so that it faces east) will be interested to learn that this one lies ENE to WSW rather than east–west, as is traditional. This may have been determined by the terrain or perhaps by a loose interpretation of what constituted east. Certainly, no one appears to have lost any sleep over it.

Visitors must first pass through a rather fine wrought-iron gate that was presented to the church in 1969 by one Wallace Menzies. A central panel contains a Celtic cross, beneath which three birds fly and three fish swim.

Inside the church, the long plain pews have been pushed to the side and the nave is filled with a series of information boards detailing the history of Canna and neighbouring Sanday (Sandaigh) from prehistoric times onwards. The well-worn wooden floor and the bare stones of the walls, many of them tinged green with mould, give the church a somewhat sad countenance. Even the paint on the modern six-sided pulpit has begun to peal, all the while defiantly crying out, 'The Word of the Lord endureth forever,' in embossed lettering. Look up and you'll see that the walls lean in to one another to form a pointed tunnel-vault over your head, but here again water damage is all too plain to see. Thankfully, the National Trust for Scotland, which owns Canna, announced in 2015 that they were seeking funds to repair the church and place Thom family memorabilia within it.

The stone-walled burial ground is home to a single solitary headstone, made of granite, which is dedicated to the memory of Allan and Johanna. The view from this point is one to be savoured. To the east of the church, on a slender 80ft-high stack, are the ruins of Coroghan Castle. The minuscule stronghold was built in the 17th century and is said to have been used by Black Donald of the Cuckoo as a prison for his second wife Marion MacLeod, whom he accused of adultery. Across the water on Sanday, a small island accessible from Canna by a bridge, stands the deconsecrated Catholic church of St Edward's, in latter years a hostel and study centre but now sadly dormant.

Before you leave Canna, it's worth visiting the island's other tiny church. A short stroll along the coast road brings you to St Columba's, a Catholic chapel built of rough stone. While the inside is disappointing – the decor appears to be modelled on a half-heartedly chintzy B&B dining room – it is one of the few churches to have begun life as a post office. 🪶

CROICK CHURCH
CROICK

Whatever their provenance, the messages scratched on the windows about the local victims of the Clearances are incredibly moving.

SPIRITUAL ORIENTATION
Church of Scotland

PHYSICAL ORIENTATION
Croick, Ardgay, Sutherland IV24 3BS
Grid reference: NH 456 914
OS Landranger map 20

PUBLIC TRANSPORT
This one is quite literally at the end of the road and there is no public transport. The church lies 10 miles along a minor road that runs west along the Strathcarron Valley from Ardgay, a village with a railway station (scotrail.co.uk; 0344 8110141).

OPENING ARRANGEMENTS
Always open.

SERVICES
3pm 2nd Sunday (May to September)
Further information: croickchurch.com; 01863 766285.

he graffiti to be found at Croick Church are a lasting reminder of one of the bleakest and most heart-rending chapters in the history of Scotland. One spring day in 1845 some 80 people wound up living temporarily in the churchyard at Croick, refugees in their own land. The curt messages scratched on the windows of the church have become their memorial, though the etchings raise more questions than perhaps they answer.

The church on which they left their plaintive mark is more remote now than it was even then. To get there, it's necessary to travel 10 miles west up the sparsely populated Strathcarron Valley, from the little village of Ardgay. The road follows the River Carron, heads off along one of its tributaries, the Blackwater, and finally dribbles away into the grass at Croick, which today consists of little more than this church and an eponymous estate. It seems a remarkable place to put a church when there is so little evidence of a potential congregation around it, but when it was completed in 1827 the communities that once flourished here filled it to overflowing. The location also had form: previously, there had been a preaching station here and, way before that, a Pictish broch (tower), of which some remains can still be seen.

If there is an air of the utilitarian about Croick Church it is because it is one of 32 identical churches built by Act of

Parliament (the snappily titled Parliamentary Act for Building Additional Places of Worship in the Highlands and Islands of Scotland) and designed by the renowned civil engineer Thomas Telford. The so-called T-plan parliamentary church (the 'T' describes the floor plan rather than referencing Telford) was the answer to a problem that seems unlikely in this day and age: one of too many Christians and not enough churches for them to attend.

Looking down on it from the road, Croick Church seems to consist of a simple nave. Even so, there is something striking about the building – if you removed the bell-cote from the western end (or added one at the eastern end), the church would be perfectly symmetrical. The white-painted north wall is punctured by two wide and almost round-arched windows flanked by two plain stone doorways fitted out with aquamarine doors. These are themselves flanked by downpipes from the guttering that issue forth into matching drains. The effect is amplified by a path that runs at a right angle to the church straight down to its centre.

It is only when you venture around the back that the rather unprepossessing vertical bar of the T is seen, topped with a clumsy looking bell-cote that looks as if it has been ripped from some larger inner-city Glaswegian kirk and shoved on top of the roof. Why there was a need for a second bell-cote at all is unclear. It's also of mild interest to note that, wherever possible, the long wall of Telford's churches faced south, whereas in this case it faces north.

As soon as you open the door (it's the one to the left) it becomes clear that Croick's reputation as the finest example of a Telford church is well deserved. The furnishings are virtually as they were when first installed. The government of the day (Lord Liverpool – he of the notorious Corn Laws – was at the helm) certainly didn't countenance the idea of wasting money on such fripperies as adornments. This is true both inside and out, and it lends the church a somewhat Puritan air.

Contrary to expectations, the long wooden pews do not face east but rather the long north wall. Separating them from the double-decker pulpit is a tremendously protracted Communion table with pews along its two long sides so that as many as possible could sit down together to take the bread and wine.

As it turned out, such generous provision became unnecessary very swiftly. Though the congregation packed the church initially, in 1843 the schism in the Church of Scotland known as the Disruption (see also Colintraive Church, p277) resulted in the members of Croick leaving en masse to form their own Free Church. Having no building to go to they conducted their worship outdoors among

the heather. A rump of about 10 locals stuck with the Church of Scotland and continued to worship at Croick, though it's easy to imagine how forlorn their services must have been.

While the Disruption clearly dealt a blow to the church, a far greater one was soon to be inflicted upon certain of its parishioners. The Highland Clearances of the 18th and 19th centuries involved the forced removal of thousands of tenant farmers from their homes and fields so that rich landowners could establish large and more profitable sheep farms in their stead. In 1845 this scourge wiped out the settlement of Glencalvie. A thriving community of subsistence farmers who could trace their tenancies in the glen to the 14th century, they had already been hit by earlier evictions that had reduced their number to 90. Now they were forced by the landlord's factor, James Gillanders, to leave their land.

A handful found land to rent elsewhere but 80 people, 23 of them children under 10, were obliged to take refuge in the churchyard, all living in one large marquee they created using poles and tarpaulins. It is not clear why they did not shelter in the church. Perhaps they considered it sacrosanct. It's unlikely that they were barred by the minister, who by all accounts was tireless in helping them.

It has been assumed that some of the exiles scratched away at the outside of the diamond-shaped panes, perhaps knowing they would never return. One states baldly 'Glencal peopl [sic] was in the churchyard here May 24 1845', while another suggests that divine retribution had caused their tribulations: 'Glencalvie people, the wicked generation Glencalvie'.

There is a certain mystery surrounding these etchings. Some give dates of 1869, 1870 and 1871, while one problematically refers to the 'Glencalvie greenyard murder' of '1854 March 31'. Stranger still, a correspondent for The Times, the erstwhile newspaper of record, noted that he could not communicate with the people because they only spoke Gaelic. If that was the case, why then are the etchings in English? Furthermore, if the group did refuse to take shelter inside the church in order not to desecrate it, wouldn't scrawling messages on the windows amount to the same thing? Taking this into account, it seems rather more likely that the Glencalvie etchings are mere reportage applied by later hands (which, if so, certainly puts the 'wicked generation' observation in a different light).

In the church there is a copy of the damning report of the clearance that appeared on 2 June in The Times. It came too late to save the people of Glencalvie, who had already left the churchyard. What became of them after they trooped sadly out of the valley, no one knows.

THE ITALIAN CHAPEL

LAMB HOLM

That a building of such elegance could be produced from such unpromising base materials inspires a real sense of wonder.

SPIRITUAL ORIENTATION
Roman Catholic

PHYSICAL ORIENTATION
Lamb Holm, Orkney
KW17 2RT
Grid reference: HY 488 006
OS Landranger map 7

PUBLIC TRANSPORT
There are many ways of getting to Lamb Holm (also known as Lambholm), a small island joined to the southeastern corner of mainland Orkney by a causeway. From mainland Scotland, take a ferry from Gills Bay to St Margaret's Hope (pentlandferries.co.uk; 0800 6888998) or embark on a longer voyage from Aberdeen to Kirkwall or Scrabster to Stromness (both northlinkferries.co.uk; 01856 885500). From whichever of these three you land at, take the X1 bus to Lamb Holm. Alternatively, cyclists can take the John O'Groats to Burwick ferry (foot passengers only; jogferry.co. uk; 01955 611353) and cycle the picturesque 13 miles to Lamb Holm, crossing various World War II causeways along the way.

OPENING ARRANGEMENTS
Open daily. For further information contact John Muir at the Italian Chapel Preservation Committee (01856 781580).

SERVICES
3.30pm 1st Sunday April to September (Mass).

n the north side of a small Orcadian island there stands a chapel that is remarkable not just for its inherent beauty but also for the exceptional circumstances under which it was built. Known simply as the Italian Chapel after the men who brought it into being, this unorthodox-looking place of worship on the isle of Lamb Holm bears testimony to both their artistry and their resourcefulness.

It's safe to say that the chapel would not exist had it not been for a disaster that occurred on 14 October 1939. On that night, German submarine *U-47* slipped into Scapa Flow and attacked the 29,000-ton HMS *Royal Oak*, which was lying at anchor. The battleship was hit by three or more torpedoes and sank in 13 minutes. There were 833 lives lost, including 126 boy sailors. In the aftermath of this catastrophe, the British government set in train one of the most ambitious engineering schemes of World War II: a series of causeways between islands to the southeast of mainland Orkney, sealing off the eastern approach to Scapa Flow and, it was hoped, keeping the anchorage safe from future U-boat raids.

With local labour at a premium, Italian prisoners-of-war were drafted in to speed up progress on what had become known as the Churchill Barriers. Since the Geneva Convention barred captured enemy servicemen from working on military projects, the authorities declared that the purpose of the causeways was to provide a land transport link between a quartet of southern isles and mainland Orkney.

The smallest and most northerly of those isles was Lamb Holm, a 95-acre plot of grass and gorse that had hitherto gone about its business in happy obscurity. It was here in January 1942 that the 13 huts of Camp 60 became home to some of the 1,200 Italian soldiers brought to Orkney to work on the barriers.

Although the prisoners built themselves a theatre and a recreation hut, they lacked a chapel. After some gentle cajoling, the camp padre Father Giacobazzi (known as Padre Giacomo) and artist Domenico Chiocchetti persuaded the camp commandant Major T P Buckland to allow the prisoners to erect a chapel in their spare time. In November 1943, the foundations were dug and two Nissen huts, joined end to end, were handed over to the prisoners. One end of the 72ft by 16ft building was to be the chapel, while the other was to function as a schoolroom.

Visit the chapel today and you'll see what an extraordinary job the Italian soldiers did. Under the guiding hand of Chiocchetti, they lined the eastern end of the conjoined Nissen huts with plasterboard, fashioned an altar out of concrete and installed windows filled with painted glass depicting St Francis of Assisi and St Catherine of Siena. A blacksmith

named Giuseppe Palumbi spent four months assiduously crafting an exquisite wrought-iron rood screen, having first built his own forge. Chiocchetti himself painted the sanctuary, allowing his prodigious artistic talent full rein. The magnificent Madonna and Child he produced as an altarpiece is the chapel's crowning glory. He based the painting on a little prayer card he carried with him for the duration of the war. Its subject was the Madonna of the Olive Branch and it was based on a painting by Italian artist Nicolò Barabino.

Such was the success they made of the eastern end that the idea of using the western end as a school was abandoned and the prisoners began transforming that too. The plasterboard lining painted by Chiocchetti and another artist called Giovanni Pennisi bears *trompe l'œil* brickwork, carved stone and ribbed ceiling effects. The rather drab exterior was given a new façade complete with bell-cote and portico created by stonemason Domenico Buttapasta from a design by Pennisi, who also sculpted a bas-relief head of Christ from red clay for the tympanum. The huts' corrugated shell was hidden beneath a layer of concrete.

Although it's difficult to believe when seeing the church up close, all the decorative materials had to be foraged. The chancel floor tiles were relieved from a German steamer called *Ilsenstein*, which had been deliberately sunk in shallow water to help form the barriers; wood for the tabernacle came from another such 'block ship'; while the rood screen and all the other fittings were made from scrap materials. Somehow, Chiocchetti managed to craft a statue of St George and the dragon from barbed wire and concrete.

The chapel had not long entered service when, on 9 September 1944 (by coincidence, the first anniversary of Italy's capitulation), the prisoners of Camp 60 were moved to a camp in Yorkshire. However, so important had the project become that Chiocchetti was allowed to stay behind to finish his work on the altar, and the Lord Lieutenant of Orkney himself vowed that the chapel would be faithfully preserved. It is as well that he did because a chapel built by prisoners at Camp 34 on nearby Burray, which pre-dated the Lamb Holm building, was demolished when the camp was cleared after the war.

The BBC paid for Domenico Chiocchetti to return to Lamb Holm in 1960 to freshen up the paintwork of his masterpiece. In a letter he wrote to the people of Orkney at the time, he declared,

The chapel is yours – for you to love and preserve. I take with me to Italy the remembrance of your kindness and wonderful hospitality… I, in leaving, leave a part of my heart.

He came back four years later, this time bearing a gift of 14 stations of the cross

which can still be seen in the chapel. Chiocchetti died in Italy in 1999, aged 89.

Bruno Volpi, a former inmate of Camp 60, summed up what many of his fellow prisoners must have felt about the chapel when he wrote to the authors of the book *Bolsters, Blocks, Barriers*:

What is it that made prisoners of war work so feverishly with partially or totally inadequate means at their disposal? It was the wish to show to oneself first, and to the world then, that in spite of being trapped in a barbed wire camp, down in spirit physically, and morally deprived of many things, one could still find something inside that could be set free.

ST BONIFACE KIRK
PAPA WESTRAY

This little kirk must be one of the nation's most strikingly located churches.

SPIRITUAL ORIENTATION
Non-denominational

PHYSICAL ORIENTATION
Papa Westray, Orkney
KW17 2BU
Grid reference: HY 488 526
OS Landranger map 5

PUBLIC TRANSPORT
This is one of the more challenging churches to get to unless you happen to be one of the 75 people living on the island of Papa Westray. From Kirkwall, on Orkney Mainland, you can either take the ferry direct to Papa Westray (orkneyferries. co.uk; 01856 872044), which typically sails twice a week, or board the more frequent (up to thrice daily) ferry to Rapness on Westray (Orkney Ferries). A minibus will then transport you to Pierowall from where the little *Golden Mariana* (Orkney Ferries again) will bear you over to Papa Westray. It's a 2.5-mile walk to the kirk, along the island's only north–south road, passing Holland Farm. The church can be seen on your left soon afterwards and is reached by a wide track.

OPENING ARRANGEMENTS
Open daily.

SERVICES
Held occasionally.

here can be few churches that boast such a dramatic and appealing location as that of St Boniface. Perched on low cliffs at the edge of a sea of pastureland, the kirk stands heroically alone, apparently attempting to command the endlessly advancing rollers of the North Atlantic below it. The sense of having arrived somewhere very special is heightened by the beauty and remoteness of Papa Westray, the compact island on which the kirk sits. Indeed, paying a visit to St Boniface Kirk feels like reaching the climax of a pilgrimage.

This has been a site of importance to Christians since the 8th century, though the current kirk dates mainly from the 12th and was enlarged around 1710. However, despite being one of only two churches in Orkney to have survived the Reformation and continued into the 20th century (the other being St Magnus Cathedral), it was abandoned in 1929 and the simple rectangular building fell into disrepair. Thankfully, it was saved from ruin and completely restored in 1993.

The kirk is unadorned but for the ziggurat-like styling of its two gables, which plants the somewhat irreverent suggestion in the viewer's mind that it has been made out of Lego. To enter, one must climb a flight of stone steps to a sea-facing

door, raised to protect the church from farm animals. Inside, the flagstoned floor speaks of great antiquity while the splendid wooden box pews, pulpit and gallery date from the Georgian enlargement. The almost Shaker-like simplicity is broken only by a small photographic display and a ceramic plaque designed by Papa Westray's children. Stepping outside into the kirkyard, a family tomb occupies the area where the kirk's chancel once stood. A little to the east of this, pilgrims can seek out a hog-backed Norse tombstone which is just about visible in the thick grass. Slabs from two Pictish crosses have also been found in the kirkyard (the Orkney Museum and the National Museum of Scotland now hold one each) – evidence that the original church was erected in the 8th century and thus may have been one of the first churches to have been dedicated to the murdered archbishop.

The eponymous St Boniface (c.675 to 754) was born in Wessex but spent a good deal of his life as a missionary to the German parts of the Frankish Empire. He was made an archbishop in 732 and founded a plethora of churches and monasteries. All went well until he took it upon himself to convert the Frisians, a people from the coast of what is now the Netherlands and Germany. Having baptised a goodly number of them, he was confronted by a local band of brigands. According to a *vita* of the saint, written soon afterwards, Boniface prevailed upon his 52 armed followers to put up no resistance 'for we are told in Scripture not to render evil for good but to overcome evil by good'. The archbishop and his entire entourage were duly slaughtered and sainthood, at least for one of the party, beckoned.

Boniface's connection with Papa Westray (known simply as Papay to Orcadians) appears to have been forged much earlier. The Pictish King Nechtan, who had already been converted, invited him to establish Christianity throughout his kingdom. The missioners often founded monasteries and churches near or on the sites of previous strongholds such as Iron Age fortified towers, so it's no surprise to find St Boniface Kirk situated close to a 5,000-year-old settlement known as the Knap of Howar.

It would be a shame to journey all the way to Papay without also venturing to St Tredwell's Loch to inspect the (admittedly scant) remnants of St Tredwell's Chapel (HY 496 509). St Tredwell, or Triduana, was a virgin said to have played some part in St Boniface's Pictish mission. Something of an unlikely saint, Triduana is reputed to have plucked out her own eyes and handed them to King Nechtan on a stick, as if proffering him some sort of ocular kebab. He appears to have done nothing to deserve this other than falling in love with her and complimenting her on her eyes.

Perversely, post mortem, the touchy saint found fame healing ophthalmic ailments. Medieval pilgrims in search of a cure for visual disorders came from far afield to pay homage to the saint and wash their eyes in the loch's waters.

The little mound on which Triduana's chapel stood can be found at the end of a stubby peninsula that juts into the loch, though all that remains now is the foundations and a scrap or two of wall. The miraculous qualities of the water are as yet unproven.

GLOSSARY

Apse

A semicircular or polygonal recess, with an arched or semi-domed roof, typically at the eastern end of a church, and usually containing the altar.

Aumbry (or ambry)

A niche or recess, fitted with a door (now often missing), in the wall near the altar, in which sacred and especially valuable objects such as the paten were kept.

Baroque

A style of decoration that prevailed in Europe at the end of the 17th and during a great part of the 18th century. It is distinguished by ornate (and some might say excessively elaborate) detail.

Bell-cote

An ornamental construction designed to contain one or two bells, and often crowned by a small spire. (Also known as a bell-turret.)

Bier

A trolley or stretcher for transporting a coffin with a corpse within.

Chancel

The section of the church, almost always at the eastern end, from which services are conducted.

Choir loft

A gallery from which a choir performs.

Consecration crosses

Incised in walls or on the altar, they mark the places that a bishop or other high-ranking cleric has anointed with holy oil to consecrate the church, thus making it fit for Christian worship.

Corbel

A piece of stone, wood or iron projecting from the vertical face of a wall to support some structure above it.

Crocket

A small carved decoration such as a bud, curled leaf or animal found on the inclined sides of pinnacles, canopies or gables.

Decorated

The style of English Gothic architecture that prevailed in the 14th century, preceded by Early English and succeeded by Perpendicular. As its name suggests, it is characterised by the use of decoration as well as a fondness for patterned stonework in windows (see 'Reticulated' below).

Diptych

A pair of paintings, usually on wooden panels, with a hinge in the middle.

Early English	Popular in the late 12th and 13th centuries, this was the first stage of English Gothic architecture and is noted for its lancet windows and pointed arches.
Finial	An ornament that caps a pinnacle, canopy, gable or similar.
Galilee	A porch or a small chapel found at the western end of a church.
Lancet	A thin vertical window or arch in the shape of a lancet.
Lath	A thin, flat and narrow strip of wood, combined with other strips to form a foundation for plaster, stucco or roofing tiles.
Mensa	A flat stone slab that forms the top surface of an altar and is usually marked with consecration crosses.
Mullion	A vertical bar in a window separating panes of glass.
Nave	The main body of a church where typically the congregation sits during a service.
Ogee	An elongated S-shaped curve.
Paten	A plate used for holding the bread during a Communion service – usually made from a precious metal such as gold or silver.
Pediment	The vertical triangular section that lies across a row of columns in a building of the Classical style.

GLOSSARY

Perpendicular   Usually known simply as Perp, this was the final stage of English Gothic (see 'Early English' and 'Decorated'). It was popular from the late 14th to mid-16th century and is notable for the vertical lines that gave the style its name. Perp churches often sport wide arches, intricate fan vaults and very large windows with thin mullions.

Piscina   A small recess in a wall, usually close to the altar, that included a basin and drain, allowing the ritual washing of vessels used in Mass.

Porticus   A side chapel or chamber projecting from the nave, typically to the north or south. The word is also sometimes applied to the entrance porch of a church.

Quatrefoil   A decoration common in tracery that resembles a four-petalled flower.

Reredos   A screen or a decorated section of wall behind the altar.

Reticulated   A net-like pattern of tracery that produces repeated geometrical shapes and often incorporates ogee curves.

Reveal   The face of an opening in a wall for a door or window.

Rood loft   The loft or platform supported by the rood screen.

Rood screen   A screen, typically of richly carved wood or stone, separating the nave from the chancel of a church.

Sanctuary	The section of the chancel that contains the altar.
Sedilia	Stone seats (usually three in a row) reserved for members of the clergy and set into the south wall of the chancel (singular: sedile).
Shingled	Wooden planks, tiles or some similar material placed in overlapping rows to cover walls or roofs.
Spandrel	The area between the outer curve of an arch and the ceiling; or the space between adjoining arches and whatever stands above them.
Stoup	A basin or font reserved for holy water, often set into a wall and normally found by the entrance door.
Stucco	Fine plaster usually comprising cement, sand, hydrated lime and water laid wet onto walls or mouldings for decorative purposes.
Surplice	A loose-fitting and almost always white garment worn over a cassock by clergy and choristers.
Tester	A flat canopy placed over a pulpit as a sounding board to project the preacher's voice out to the congregation.
Tracery	Ornamental stonework, often seen in the upper portion of a Gothic window.
Transept	Either of two sections that project at right angles from the eastern end of the nave to form a cross-shaped floor plan.
Trefoil	A decoration containing three rounded lobes like a clover leaf, used in medieval tracery and often appearing in the upper part of windows.
Triptych	Three paintings, usually on wood, with the outer panels hinged to the central one, and often serving as an altarpiece.
Tympanum	A recessed triangular space within a pediment that is often decorated with sculpture.
Undercroft	A room beneath a church or chapel.
Vault	A roof formed of an arch or arches.

SELECT BIBLIOGRAPHY

BOOKS

Bolsters, Blocks, Barriers, Alastair and Anne Cormack, The Orkney View, 1992

Discovering the Smallest Churches in Scotland, John Kinross, The History Press, 2010

England's 1000 Best Churches, Simon Jenkins, Allen Lane, 1999

Orkney's Italian Chapel, Philip Paris, Black & White Publishing, 2013

Penguin Dictionary of Saints, Donald Attwater, Penguin Books, 1965

St Margaret Queen of Scotland and her Chapel, Lucy Menzies, Ronald A Knox, Ronald Selby Wright, St Margaret's Chapel Guild, 2012

The Observer's Book of Old English Churches, Lawrence E Jones, Frederick Warne & Co, 1965

While researching the English churches I also referred to the series of county-by-county architectural guides entitled *The Buildings of England* edited and often written or co-written by Sir Nikolaus Pevsner and published by Penguin from 1951 onwards.

Compiling the glossary, I found myself charmed by a wonderful multi-volume opus called *The Century Dictionary of the English Language: An Encyclopædic Lexicon*, edited by William Dwight Whitney and published by The Century Co. of New York in 1889.

I am very grateful for the permission granted by Alastair and Anne Cormack to quote from their book *Bolsters, Blocks, Barriers*, and by John E Vigar to use a passage from his guide to the Old Church of St Mary the Virgin, Preston Candover.

OTHER LITERATURE

I am indebted to the authors of the many leaflets, guides, articles and information boards I have come across during my visits to the churches in this book. Reading them I have often come to an awareness that I am gleaning knowledge won at the expense of considerable time and effort spent wading through reams of official records in dusty back rooms, tracking down books with obscure titles, and mining the memories of elderly parishioners – all to render their accounts as faithful to the history of their respective churches as is humanly possible.

All too often this selfless work goes unthanked, and in many instances entirely uncredited. Where I have been able to ascertain the identity of an author of a guide or article, I have included it below. My thanks go out to you all, whether known or unknown, and I beg that anyone whose name I have inadvertently overlooked will accept my apologies.

Anthony Barnes (St Andrew's, Frenze)

Charles K Burton & Gerald L Matthews (St Michael de Rupe, Brentor)

Lawrence Butler (St Peter's, Cambridge)

Rev David L Cawley (St Thomas Becket, Fairfield)

Derek Cotterill (St Oswald's, Widford)

Dr Simon Cotton (St Mary's, Barton Bendish)

Walter Godfrey, Cecil Piper & Frank Fox-Wilson (Church of the Good Shepherd, Lullington)

Dr John Gray (Colintraive Church, Colintraive)

Bruce Jamieson (St Peter's, Linlithgow)

Sonya Linskaill (St Fillan's, Killin)

P A MacNab (Croick Church, Croick)

Dr Richard K Morris (All Saints, Billesley)
Brian Payne (Guyhirn Chapel, Guyhirn)
Canon Arthur Reid (St Issui's, Patricio)
Bron Roberts (Friends Meeting House,
    Dolobran)
David Scott (St Swithun-upon-Kingsgate,
    Winchester)
Kenneth Smith (St Edwold's, Stockwood)
Henry Stapleton (St Mary's, Lead)
Rev G Ivor Thomas (St Ina's, Llanina)
Gerald Tyler (St Leonard's, Chapel-le-Dale)
John E Vigar (Old Church of St Mary the
    Virgin, Preston Candover)
Wing Commander John Wynne (St Tanwg's,
    Llandanwg)

WEBSITES

Again, I am beholden to a great number
of people who have faithfully hosted or
contributed to the websites that have helped
me in my research. Where a church has a
dedicated website, I have listed its address
in the information section for that church.
Other websites that I found useful are
included here:

Cadw: *cadw.gov.wales*
Churches Conservation Trust:
    visitchurches.org.uk
Church in Wales: *churchinwales.org.uk*
Church of England: *churchofengland.org*
Early British Kingdoms:
    earlybritishkingdoms.com
English Heritage: *english-heritage.org.uk*
Farne Islands: *nationaltrust.org.uk*
Friends of Friendless Churches:
    friendsoffriendlesschurches.org.uk
Monkton Rectorial Benefice:
    revjones.fsnet.co.uk
Norfolk Churches: *norfolkchurches.co.uk*
Norman Chapel, Durham:
    durhamworldheritagesite.com;
    rwromanesque.co.uk & *dur.ac.uk*
St Margaret's Chapel Guild:
    stmargaretschapel.com
Scotland's Churches Trust:
    scotlandschurchestrust.org.uk
Undiscovered Scotland:
    undiscoveredscotland.co.uk

AUTHOR'S ACKNOWLEDGEMENTS

One of the joys of being a travel writer is that I get to meet a wide range of people, the vast majority of whom brighten my life in some way. While researching this book I have been fortunate to receive a great deal of help from a great many luffly individuals. The following have been particularly obliging:

Alan Fitzpatrick (St Trillo's)
Alexa Forbes (various Glos and Wilts churches)
Briony Jones at asapventures.co.uk
Caroline and Eilidh Delves (St Thomas Becket, Fairfield)
Claire Lillie at Arriva Trains Wales
David Harris and his mother (St Michael de Rupe)
Donna Wood (Old Church of St Mary the Virgin, Preston Candover)
Erin Clark (St Peter's, Cambridge)
Gemma Lewis at Durham Castle
Grant Thomson and Nigel the guide, both at Edinburgh Castle
Hayley Hewitt (various Welsh churches)
Hazel Wills (various churches)
Hilda Walter (Our Lady and St Anne's)
James Davis at Great Western Railway
Janet Christopher (St Mary's, Snibston)
John Adams (St Tanwg's)
Kim and Nick Hoare at Ivy Grange Farm, Suffolk
Lucy Wright at Abellio Greater Anglia
Michelle Wayper and Mike Francis (St Ethelburga's, Great Givendale)
Paul Cottle (Our Lady and St Anne's)
Philip and Joanne (St Mary of the Angels, Brownshill)
Rev Canon Roger Jones and Rev Geoffrey Howell (St Govan's)
Rev Christine Barclay (St Peter's, Linlithgow)
Richard Salkeld at Virgin East Coast
Susan Booth (St Tanwg's)
Susanna Wallace (Little Gidding)
The good ladies of St Augustine's, Sookholme, both for their welcome and their recommendation of Steetley Chapel
Tracy Clifton at Virgin Trains

I would also like to thank the many, many people who took time to answer my questions, no matter how foolish or naïve they might have been; who let me bother them for keys to churches or made special journeys to let me in themselves; or who were helpful or encouraging in other ways.

I'd like to make special mention of Tom Jones at the Churches Conservation Trust (CCT – visitchurches.org.uk). Several of the entries in this book are cared for by the CCT, a charitable organisation that does a fine job looking after 300 churches throughout England. Although no regular services take place in CCT churches, they remain consecrated.

Likewise, I thank Matthew Saunders at the Friends of Friendless Churches (FFC – friendsoffriendlesschurches.org.uk), a body that has rescued 40 redundant historic churches in England and Wales.

As is the case with any of the other churches in this book, any donation you might make to the CCT or FFC would be most welcome.

I'm also very grateful to the people at carrentals.co.uk who helped me reach those churches that were too remote even for my willing cycling legs.

My particular thanks go to Mike and Lorna Houston for putting me up and, indeed, putting up with me for much of the time I was researching this book.

I'm also extremely grateful to Mark, Jude, Seth and Silas Woolley, in whose Yorkshire caravan two-thirds of this book was written; and to Richard and Michèle Kummrow, in whose delightful house on Lake Geneva the other third took on flesh. Authors, eh? Their lives are rubbish.

I'm indebted to Harriet Yeomans for drawing the church cutaway and to James Tims for overseeing design matters.

I'd like to thank my literary agents, Ben Mason and Michael Alcock at Johnson and Alcock (yes, get me, I've got two agents, and a telly agent as well – if you've got people too we'll get yours to speak to mine).

And last but certainly not least, I send thanks to my wonderful editors at the AA, Helen Brocklehurst and Donna Wood, not only for editing this book and others before it, but for being such excellent coves.

PICTURE CREDITS

AA Media wishes to thank the following illustrators, photographers and organisations for their assistance in the preparation of this book.

Abbreviations for the picture credits are as follows – (t) top; (b) bottom; (l) left; (r) right; (c) centre

Cover and map illustrations by David Wardle
Features of a church illustration by Harriet Yeomans

23 Loop Images Ltd/Alamy Stock Photo; 60 James Tims; 75 David Lyon/Alamy Stock Photo; 89 Jack Thurston; 90 Jack Thurston; 141 Liquid Light/Alamy Stock Photo; 142 Colin Underhill/ Alamy Stock Photo; 193 Ashley Cooper/Alamy Stock Photo; 194 Ashley Cooper/Alamy Stock Photo; 206 Chris Howes/Wild Places Photography/Alamy Stock Photo; 207 David Parker/ Alamy Stock Photo; 208 Chris Howes/Wild Places Photography/Alamy Stock Photo; 209 Chris Howes/Wild Places Photography/Alamy Stock Photo; 222 Ian G Dagnall/Alamy Stock Photo; 250 Christopher McGowan/Alamy Stock Photo; 256 PearlBucknall/Alamy Stock Photo; 268 JOHN KELLERMAN/Alamy Stock Photo; 269 McPhoto/Ingo Schulz/Alamy Stock Photo; 270l Alexei Fateev/Alamy Stock Photo; 270r robertharding/Alamy Stock Photo; 271 Hemis/Alamy Stock Photo; 289-292 Undiscovered Scotland; 303 SJ Images/Alamy Stock Photo; 304 Tim Gainey/Alamy Stock Photo; 306 tatòkada/Stockimo/Alamy Stock Photo; 307 Tim Gainey/Alamy Stock Photo; 309 Doug Houghton/Alamy Stock Photo; 310 orkneypics/Alamy Stock Photo.

All other photographs taken by Dixe Wills.

Every effort has been made to trace the copyright holders, and we apologise in advance for any unintentional omissions or errors. We would be pleased to apply any corrections in a following edition of this publication.